In the name of God

***

Unwithering Flames: Book-4 "Shaheed Mudeq; Narrated by His Wife" by: Maryam Baradaran
Copyright © 2023 Green Palm

All rights reserved. No portion of this book may be reproduced in any form without permission from the publisher. For permissions contact: info@greenpalm.net
Translated and edited by: Green Palm books
Cover by Hossein Reza Vanaki
First Edition

To contribute towards future publications and be informed of the other books in the collection, please contact: info@Greenpalm.net

Unwithering Flames

— Book 4 - Manouchehr Mudeq —

In order to have a fruitful and prosperous relationship, people have come to terms that they must love one another. Unfortunately, the meaning of true love has been lost. Many have relegated love to mere intimacy between a man and a woman. However, this is just the initial stage of true love, and we must aspire to reach a higher level beyond physical attraction. Such love is built on the foundation of honesty, enjoyment, selflessness, and spiritual attainment. Although many strive to reach this transcendent form of love, the affairs of this world become a barrier for them.

This series of books, entitled Unwithering Flames, recounts to us stories of those men and women who n the events of the Islamic Revolution and the Iraq's war against Iran turned away from this world just for the sake of God. In doing so, they became lovers in the true sense. They had the kind of love that did not just make the pain of this world bearable, rather it was something beautiful for them. The love whose flame has not dimmed even with martyrdom or death.

🌐 www.GREENPALM.net
✈️📞 +98 999 99 16 140
✉️ info@GREENPALM.net

SYNOPSIS

The love story of Fereshteh and Manouchehr began during the endless anxious time of the Islamic Revolution. It all began one day when Manouchehr rode his motorcycle to rescue Fereshteh from the hands of the Shah's police officers, who had surrounded her.

A war broke out only a couple of months after beginning their new life. Iraq had thrown the first stone toward Iran, and Manouchehr was not one to stay at home with his revolutionary spirit. Knowing that the time would come soon where he would have to leave, he spent his every waking moment with Fereshteh. Their hearts had become intertwined with each other's.

Chemical wounds of her husband were the remaining memories of the war, for this love-struck lady, and now it was time for her to summon all her might in order to withstand the difficulties of life beyond the war; all of the unkindness, the harshness of his words, the financial difficulties, and above all, the breaths of a Manouchehr who no longer wished to be in this world. However, his enchanted heart would not allow him to leave.

To this day, Fereshteh regrets her momentary look of consent to allow Manouchehr to leave this world, and thus, he closed his eyes for the last time and escaped this world. Fereshteh, however, can still feel his presence whenever she hears the greetings of her son Ali, whenever she sees the patience of her daughter Hoda, and especially so, whenever she sees a white pigeon at her window.

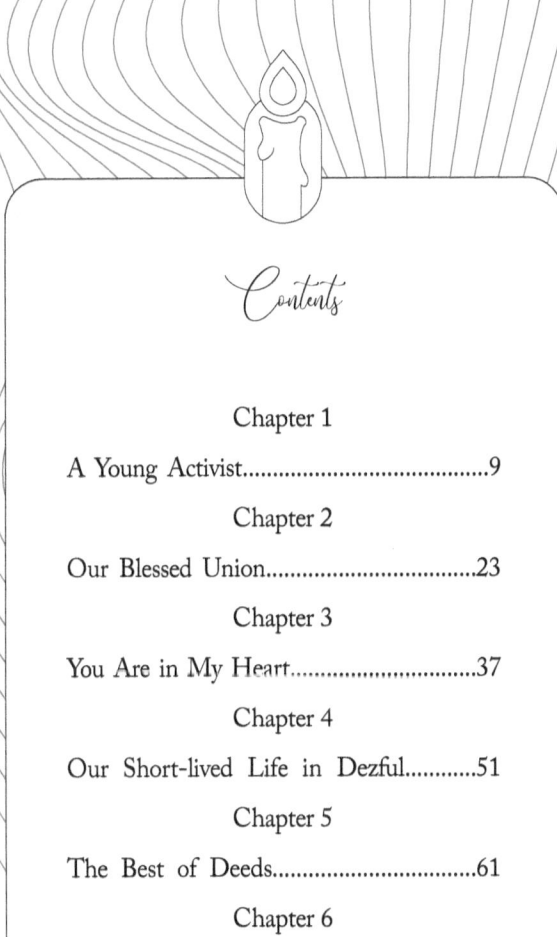

Contents

Chapter 1
A Young Activist..........................9

Chapter 2
Our Blessed Union....................23

Chapter 3
You Are in My Heart................37

Chapter 4
Our Short-lived Life in Dezful............51

Chapter 5
The Best of Deeds....................61

Chapter 6
A Victim of Chemical Weapons..............73

Chapter 7
White Pigeon.........................101

Chapter 1

A Young Activist

She had all that a child her age could wish for. She was allowed to go wherever she wanted and to do whatever she wanted. Despite this, she still had a dream that would remain; she wished to put a tray full of bamieh[1] on her head and sell them on the street. This was the only wish which her father was reluctant to fulfill. She was sometimes muttering about how they deprived her of this pleasure. But one night, her father bought a tray full of bamieh and said to Fereshteh, "Sell these to us at home." She had no other wishes to be granted.

---

1. *Bamieh* is a kind of Iranian sweet made of flour, oil, and sugar.

My father always supported us. Everything was ready at the drop of a hat. I grew up in a family of four sisters and two brothers. Fariba, who married Jamshid, Manouchehr's brother, a year after my marriage, Faranak, Fahimeh, Fariborz, Mohsen, and I.

We all had freedom at home. "You can do whatever you want; however, just lead a well-lived life," my father always told us. At the age of fifteen, around 1977, I started reading books for pleasure. There were plenty of factions and parties that I wanted to know more about. I didn't like the books of the ÷ party.[2] I felt close to God in my heart and loved Him endlessly. I couldn't believe that God doesn't exist. I couldn't fight with my soul and my heart. Finally, I decided to cut them out. The books of *Munafiqin*[3] included

---

2. In Iranian literature, "Tudeh'i" refers to a member of the Tudeh Party, the biggest socialist party in Iran, which was directly associated with the Soviet Union.
3. People's Mojahedin Organization (MEK), known in Iran as Munafiqin (Hypocrites), is a scandalous terrorist group that fled Iran in 1981, because of its conflicts with the religious beliefs of the Iranian people and the government, resulting in widespread assassinations and slaughters of the Iranian people and the officials of the Islamic Republic of Iran.

a lot of stories about the tortures tolerated by them in prison of Shah.[4] Their writings were unappealing, so I decided to first learn about Islam properly before studying any other school of thought. On the pretext of doing homework, I read Dr. Shariati's[5] books with my friends. Gradually, I decided to wear *hijab*.[6] My mother didn't prefer the *chador*.[7] I asked her to sew me a *chador* for when I would visit the holy shrines with my friends. I always folded my *chador* and put it

---

4. Mohammad Reza Pahlavi (1919-1980), the last Shah of Iran. He succeeded his father in 1941, and ruled Iran for thirty-seven years under the supervision of the United Kingdom and then the United States of America. The political, economic, and moral corruption of the Shah and his household is well-known in the history of Iran.

5. Dr. Ali Shariati (1933-1977) was a well-known Iranian intellectual and a theorist of anti-colonialism, who tried to call the youths to an authentic version of Islam focused on its social and political dimensions.

6. The term *hijab* is mainly used to refer to a religious covering in the presence of non-mahram men. To maintain *hijab*, women must cover their body and adornments from non-mahram men.

7. A *chador* is a long cloak-like garment, which covers the entire body, worn by Muslim women in Iran and some other countries in public places.

at the bottom of my bag and covered it with a pile of books. When I went out, I wore it until I returned home. Wearing *chador* was considered a political issue at that time. My family did not want me to become a political activist. "You see the fuss, I see the end," my father used to say. But I had already become a revolutionist. I knew that this regime was to fall.

The backdoor of our school opened to a boy's high school, so we could exchange Imam's (Imam Khomeini) manifestos and records with the aid of some of the boys. The janitor of the school helped us as well. I remember the first time I listened to one of the Imam's speeches; I fell for his voice more than his words. He was just like us. I could understand his colloquial words and sweet accent. I thought that I was doing all these things secretly. I was careful not to reveal myself at home.

> *Father knew that Fereshteh was up to something. Fereshteh and her sister, Fariba, were studying in the same school. Fariba knew that Fereshteh ditched school early and went out with her friends. She let father know about it, but he took it on the chin. He just wanted to send Fereshteh away from*

Tehran, or to send her to Ahvaz[8] or Arak[9] to his relative's house. "Good, I can get my work done easier in Arak or Ahvaz, since they are small cities," Fereshteh thought. Wherever they would send her, she had more freedom.

She was vibrant and passionate everywhere that she was sent to go. Moreover, her father didn't know what Fereshteh was up to! Whenever there was something happening, she was the first person there, she didn't miss any rallies. She and her friends acted as security guards. Even he did not know that at 7th November's rally, she was very close to getting caught.

On November 7, the guards of the Shah prohibited people from demonstrating. We tried to escape but the guards chased after us. They took my *chador* and scarf off and

---

8. Ahvaz is a major historical city in Iran and the capital of Khuzestan Province in southwestern Iran. It was the main headquarters of the Iranian army in the Iraqi war on Iran. It was a target of frequent missile and air strikes of the Iraqi army.

9. Arak is a populated industrial city in Iran, located near Qom.

started to hit me around my waist with their batons. Suddenly, a motorcyclist, who was passing by, took my elbow and dragged me on his motorcycle. My feet were dragging on the ground, and my shoes were about to come off. He stopped after passing some alleys. There were many manifestos hidden in my clothes, some of which were visible.

"Do you have manifesto[10] papers?" he asked. He had a helmet on his head, so I was unable to see his face. "Yes, I do," I said.

"Which group do you belong to?" he asked.

"What do you mean by 'which group'?! These are Imam's manifesto papers," I replied.

He took off his helmet and asked again, "Do you distribute Imam's manifesto notes?"

---

10. Since November 1964 to February 1979, the Pahlavi regime exiled Imam Khomeini to Najaf and then France. During this period, he issued manifestos in which he expressed his position and led people's campaigns against the Pahlavi regime. The Pahlavi regime had criminalized any duplication or distribution of Imam Khomeini's manifestos.

I felt insulted. What was wrong with me? Why couldn't I do this?

"Why are you doing this while Imam's words have not influenced you? Why have you come to a demonstration like this?" he said. Then he turned his head away. I looked at myself. I had not covered my head with anything. But this was not unconventional back then. My clothes were messed up as well.

He raised his hand to get the manifesto papers, but I didn't give them up. "I will turn you in," he said. I was frightened, so I gave him the papers. He returned one of the papers and said, "Go read it. Pursue these matters only if you understand them."

I could not be indifferent to his words. "Are you a true follower of Imam Khomeini? Hasn't Imam told you not to prejudge? First, see what has happened and then speak; I had a *chador* and scarf, but those guards snatched it from me," I said. "Really?" he said, and I replied, "Why should I lie to you? Who do you think you are?"

He gave the papers back to me and told me to stay put until he came back. But I followed him to see where he was going and what he was up to. He along with some of his biker buddies went to where the rally was being held, and they beat up a few of the guards and crashed some of their car windows. Then he brought back my *chador* and scarf that were left there. I didn't want him to know that I had chased him. I started to run to the place where I was supposed to wait, but he got there sooner. He gave the scarf and *chador* and said, "They should know not to take a Muslim woman's *chador*."

He took the papers, "The path you have chosen is dangerous. Take care of yourself, young lady," he said, and then he left.

> *"Young lady!" After all that ranting and raving, he called her "young lady"; a girl whom everyone had to handle with kiddie gloves. She shook her chador and tied up her scarf firmly. She didn't know why but she liked the boy. She wasn't ordered at home what to wear, who to go with, what to read, and what to see. But the boy had blamed her for her chador. His words were bitter; however, he had won her heart.*

Later, it hit me who he was. He was Manouchehr, our neighbor's son, but I had never seen him before. My family had a close relationship with his family. I had heard his name, but I hadn't seen him. I saw him yet again on 10th February. We grabbed some guns from the Police College. I put some G-3 guns on my shoulder and some bandoleers around my neck. The streets were entrenched. We jumped from roof to roof and passed dozens of them. We went to the street near the sixth police station on Gorgan Street. It was entrenched too. We handed whatever we had brought to the guys. Manouchehr was also there. He had covered his face with a *chafiyeh*.[11] I could just see his eyes. "Is that you again?" he asked.

He took the cartridges and laughed, "What are these? Should they be thrown by hand?" he asked.

I had brought DShK bullets. I thought they might come in handy because they were big. "If you don't need them, I will take them elsewhere," I said. "No, no, I appreciate it; just leave here now," he said.

---

11. *Chafiyeh* is a checkered and often white headdress worn by men to protect the head, eyes, and mouth against the sun, sand, etc. Iranian warriors had *chafiyehs* with them during the Iraq Ba'ath regime's war on Iran.

> *She couldn't be indifferent to those two visits. She desired to know that boy, the boy who lifted her like a leaf and saved her neck, and taunted her all the time. She did not even know his name. Why was she thinking about the boy all the time? Maybe just out of curiosity, she had a strange feeling about him. She convinced herself that she will not see him anymore. It was better to forget him, but he was in her mind, more or less.*

I wasn't infatuated by him; it was not like I was thinking about him all the time and not eating anything, but Manouchehr was the first man who came in my life: the first and the last man. I was never obsessed with love. I didn't know who he was and where he was.

After the revolution, I busied myself with my education. I became the head of the school council. I enjoyed being a part of that more than studying. In the summer, my friend, Maryam, and I enrolled in tailoring and English language classes.

One day, we wanted to go to the tailoring class. While I was leaving home, the phone rang. Somebody wanted to talk to Latifeh, our neighbor, who lived in the opposite house. They did not have a telephone line, so I went to call her. The door was half open, and I went in. I saw Manouchehr sitting on the steps and smoking. I forgot why I went there. I looked at him, and he stared back at me up until the moment he stood and went in. While Manouchehr was entering the room, Latifeh came, "Sweetie, can I help you?" she asked.

I told her somebody was waiting for her on the phone. She called Manouchehr and said she was going to answer the phone. Manouchehr was Latifeh's son. "Where are you going?" Latifeh asked me. "To my tailoring class," I replied.

"Wait. Manouchehr will drop you off at your class." That day, Manouchehr drove us to the class. We didn't say a word to each other; it was unexpected. I thought that I would not see him again, let alone be in the same neighborhood as him. At the weekend, our families went to Fasham[12] together, to my father's garden.

Her father and Manouchehr were sitting next to each other and talking

---

12. Fasham is a small city in the north of Tehran.

quietly. She found a long stick, put it on her shoulder, and called the kids to take them to the riverside. Manouchehr followed them. The kids were playing in the river. Fereshteh leaned against the stick, sat on a rock and put her hands in the water. Manouchehr stood in front of her with his hand on his chest, "I want to go to Paveh,[13] I cannot sit idly," he said. "So, don't stay!" Fereshteh said. "I do not know how to say it," he said. She wanted people to talk plainly. She hated to beat around the bush, particularly, when her future partner in life was talking to her. He had to be able to swallow his pride. "So, first go learn how to say it, and then come to me," Fereshteh said. Manouchehr stroked his hair. He was at a loss for words. He stayed for some moments and then left.

My father asked me a couple of times, "Fereshteh! did Manouchehr say anything

---

13. Paveh is an ancient Kurdish border town in Iran, in Kermanshah Province. It was a center of conflicts during the Kurdistan riots, which was liberated from the siege of riot forces, under the commandership of Shaheed Mustafa Chamran.

to you?" I always replied, "No. How come?" And he would say, "Nothing. Just asking."

He had asked for my father's permission to talk to me. My father liked and trusted Manouchehr a lot. Even after knowing that Manouchehr had fallen in love with me, he let us go steady. "I trust Manouchehr more than my eyes," he said.

Most of the time, while Maryam and I were leaving for our class, Manouchehr would be returning home from work. We used to meet each other in front of the door, and he would give us a ride to the class. Once, he locked the car doors from the inside and didn't let me get out. "If you do not listen to my words, I will not let you go," he said.

"Your words must be from the bottom of your heart, then I will listen to them," I said. Manouchehr started to talk, "If this revolution needs me and if I need you, I will choose the revolution and my country and then my feelings, but I love you," he continued, "I will not hinder your studies, work or activities, provided that you won't hinder mine either," he said. "Let me approve of you first, then you may put forth any conditions," I said. He went as red as a beetroot. I took a glance at the mirror of the car. His eyes were full of tears. I could not bear it, "If I answer, wouldn't you think that I was being too eager?" He looked at me in the mirror. "I have been waiting for your words for a long time," I said. He could not believe it. Then he unlocked the doors, and I got out. He moved his head closer, "Since when?" he asked. "Since the 10th of February," I replied.

Chapter 2

Our Blessed Union

Manouchehr was thrilled to bits. He then hit the gas pedal and left as fast as he could. He even forgot to say goodbye to her. She smiled. Why did she reveal those things to him? She just knew that her father would be happy, maybe happier than her. But she was on edge because she was only sixteen years old, and that occasion was unprecedented in her family. Her mother had married at twenty. Whenever there was a suitor, her mother used to say that her daughters would not marry before the age of twenty-five. In a situation like this, Fereshteh said, "Our parents will not let us get married!" and then shook her mother's shoulder to make her

> *laugh. Those words were just a joke, but they were going to be serious. She was scared. Life had a lot of responsibilities, and she did not know what to do.*

I did not even know how to cook. After our marriage, the first dish that I cooked was *istambuli*.[14] I asked my mother on the phone how to cook it, but it did not go well and came out like soup. Although it was watery, Manouchehr ate it and even praised it. However, I was reluctant to eat. The next day, I made meatballs, but they were more like rocks rather than food. Manouchehr had prepared the table, and he was playing marbles with them. He laughed and said, "I have to tolerate my wife's cooking and even eat rocks until she learns." He said to me, "Cook them one by one carefully, and you will get the hang of it."

The day that Manouchehr's family came to propose, my father said to me, "Don't you know?! Manouchehr's parents have come here to ask for our blessing on your marriage." Manouchehr had not come. My

---

14. *Istambuli polo* is a popular Iranian dish made with rice and tomato. The dish has a Turkish origin.

father had seen through the window that Manouchehr was performing his prayers. My mother requested a week to inform them of our final decision. I had a rich and educated suitor already, but Manouchehr was an uneducated person. He had left high school to work in an automobile repair shop. He came from an average-class family. They did not even own their own house. Everybody who heard about this, remarked, "You are crazy. Are you going to live in a room? Who likes this?" However, I would do it because I had fallen for him.

One week became one month. We met each other frequently. He was worried. It was difficult for both of us to be surrounded by uncertainty. After a month, he lost his patience, "I want to go to Kurdistan, Paveh, let me know where I stand. Fereshteh, what should I do?" he said.

Manouchehr was a forbearing person, but his impatience regarding this particular matter made me restless too. I consulted my family, and my uncles disagreed. "If you disagree, I will go to the notary public office with my father, and I will marry Manouchehr. I just want a holy Quran and a piece of *shakheh nabat*[15] as my dowry," I said. But because my father insisted, I accepted 110 thousand tomans[16] as my dowry to avoid people's remarks. However, Manouchehr's father raised it to 150 thousand tomans. We got engaged on Eid al-Adha.[17]

Manouchehr stared at Fereshteh and said, "Who sacrificed now?" He couldn't keep up with her ready wit. So, Fereshteh turned to him and said, "You don't need to think about it much. It is obvious, I made the sacrifice." He burst into laughter. Fereshteh took the necklace which Manouchehr gave her as an engagement gift, and turned it around to see the engraved words, "10th February 1977." If Manouchehr's words were so pleasing on that day, his

---

15. *Shakheh nabaat* (similar to rock candy) is a kind of confection with branch-like crystals. It is a common practice among Iranians to put a number of *shakheh nabaats* among the decorations of the engagement cermony, as a symbol of love between the couple.

16. Toman is the *Iranian* currency.

17. Eid-e Qurban or Eid al-Adha (Holiday of Sacrifice) is Dhu l-Hijjah 10 in the Islamic calendar. This is one of the major Eids (holidays) of the Muslims.

presence was even more precious and beautiful. Manouchehr was her dream man, a trustworthy, loving, and brave man.

While I had acrophobia, he was crazy about heights and flying. He couldn't believe that I was scared of heights. "How does a girl fear heights, while carrying some G3 guns, DHsk bandoleer, and jumps over lots of roofs?" he asked.

We used to go hiking and get on ski lifts in the mountains. On these ski lifts, I was reciting the Quran so much out of fear, I may have memorized the whole Quran! He took me to a motorcycle race field and hang gliding. If we wanted to watch a movie, we would watch documentaries on the war in Cuba and the revolution of Algeria. He gave me lots of books, especially historical ones. We used to read them together. Even though he left school himself, he encouraged me to continue my studies. His father wanted him to continue his studies, but he did not. His father made him work in an automobile repair shop to learn the harsh reality of life. So, Manouchehr ditched school and started to work. Because of this, he insisted on me continuing my studies. He used to sit and watch me study. We liked to be next to each other all the time, not just when we were talking, but even when we were silent.

We rented a house in our neighborhood. On the birthday of Imam Mahdi (a),[18] we held a wedding party. It was close to my exams, and I had to study at night. He always helped me with my studies. After my exams, we went to the north of Iran on our honeymoon, which lasted one and a half months. Wherever we liked, we put up our tent and camped. We had just started our new life as a couple when the war began.

It was early in October. While we were having lunch, we heard on the radio that the government had summoned the people who were serving as soldiers in 1977, to go to the battlefield. "Who are they referring to?" I asked. "People who had served their military service in 1977," he replied. Whilst I was checking the date that Manouchehr served his military service, Rasoul, his brother, suddenly came in and they went out

---

18. Imam al-Mahdi, al-Hujjah (b. 255/869), is the twelfth Shiite Imam who is in occultation, and the Shias wait for his reappearance. According to the Shias, he is the promised savior who appears in the end time and will fill the world with justice.

together. He returned in the afternoon with a grey backpack in his hands. Having seen him, I said, "Why did you take this?"

"I will need this. Get dressed. We want to go out with Maryam and Rasoul," he said. Maryam was my friend who was newly engaged to Rasoul.

We went to Farahzad.[19] Sitting around the table, Manouchehr said, "We will set out tomorrow."

"What? Why so early?" I said.

"We are among those who have to go," he said.

"What do you mean by 'we'?" Maryam asked.

"My brother, Rasoul and I," he replied.

Maryam started to nag, "Rasoul, no. You cannot go. We have just gotten engaged. What will I do if something goes wrong?" she said. I was as sick as a parrot, but I preferred not to say anything, because I wanted to keep her spirits up. They had been engaged for only two months.

---

19. Farahzad is a neighborhood in North West Tehran in which some traditional restaurants are located.

> *She could not sleep a wink, so she looked at Manouchehr's eyes. She never found out what color they were: brown, hazel or green, as if they were changing their color. She grabbed his hands and touched his fingers. She forced a smile on her lips. His two thumbs were not similar in shape. One of them was wider than the other. It was crushed by a hammer. Manouchehr said, "Everyone has two thumbs, I have a thumb and a super-thumb!" She wanted to keep all those moments in her mind. She would need them. Manouchehr said, "There is just one thing which can separate us; another love, and that is my love for God, nothing else."*
>
> *She held back her sobs, put her head on his hands, and said, "Promise that you will write to me." But Manouchehr did not like writing. Moreover, there was no opportunity to write on the battlefield. She said quietly, "At least a sentence." Manouchehr gave her hands a squeeze and promised her to write as soon as he could.*

Later, he wrote many letters, but I missed him even more when I received his letters or heard his voice. I always felt his absence.

Rasoul and Manouchehr's other friends brought the letters from the battlefield. Also, they delivered my letters and other things to him. Rasoul was a chemical engineer and had to commute to Tehran every once in a while, for his job.

We went to the garrison in two cars. Manouchehr stood beside me and gave a pat on my father's back, then kissed his mother. He did not want to leave us, but he had to go.

At noon, they got on a bus and went away. Returning home alone was very hard for me, and because of this it was the last time that I saw him off. Maryam accompanied me home. She was crying loudly, and I was dejected and forlorn. I was trying not to cry loudly. When I arrived home, I felt like I had pins and needles everywhere; my arms and legs were numb. I thought that Manouchehr was no longer mine and it made me fearful.

After his first deployment, Manouchehr did not come back for six months. I was in my senior year of high school, but I no longer had any passion to go to classes, so I just took the exams. I had busied myself with *basij*[20] `and paramedical services. My friends and I used to go to the Khanevadeh Hospital to help injured soldiers that were taken there. One day, I visited a wounded soldier who was injured by a shrapnel shell in his hip, and the bone of his hand had pierced his right side. I said to my friend, "For the time being, I can take care of this man, but who will look after Manouchehr?" My spirit dropped when I was observing that scene, so I did not go to the hospital anymore.

> *Where was Manouchehr? How was he? She suddenly took a glance at some fresh narcissus flowers in the hands of an old man, who was moving among the cars to sell them. It was just last year that Fereshteh and Manouchehr were walking with each other over here. She couldn't take her eyes off the flowers. At*

---

20. *Basij* consists of volunteer forces who were formed in Iran during the Iraq-Iran war, alongside the Islamic Revolutionary Guard Corps and the Army of the Islamic Republic of Iran in defense of Iran against its Ba'ath enemy. After the war, this force still plays a role in various fields in which widespread participation of people or public services are required.

that moment, Manouchehr called her many times, but she did not hear him. Manouchehr noticed that the flowers had drawn her attention. He bought all of them for her! He always gave her some narcissus flowers, sometimes even a couple of bouquets a day. He used to say, "These flowers like coldness, like you!" But that year, the weather was bitter cold. Everything was dismal to her eyes. Sunrise, sunset, cloudy weather; all of these were making her upset. New Year[21] was coming up, but she was feeling under the weather.

I like February and March, because everything becomes fresh and new, and I evolve too. It was as if there was an upheaval in my parent's house. Although that year I was at my own house for the first time, I did nothing. My mother and my sisters, along with Manouchehr's mother and his sister, came to my home to help me with the housecleaning.

On New Year's Eve, everybody wanted to take me to their home, but I did not go, and I did not let them stay at my home either.

---

21. Persian new year starts at the first day of spring.

I set a sheet on the floor and began to read the Holy Quran. Then I went through my family albums and fell asleep on the sheet. Suddenly, I woke up at 3:30 a.m. Someone was knocking on the window. As soon as I opened the door, a fluffy doll fell on my face. It was a white teddy-bear with some flowers in its hand. It was Manouchehr. He had come to me, but with a muddy and terrible appearance. He was dusty from head to toe. Generally, he was a neat person, but on the battlefield, he could take a bath only once in a blue moon. I washed his hair for an hour to get rid of the dust. An hour later, he got out of the bath and then, we sat by the *sofreh*.[22] He unzipped his bag and gave me some souvenirs. He had found a lot of marbles with various shapes, which he had strained with sandpaper. Some poems, with my name and his, were engraved on them. There were some unsent letters in his bag, which he told me to read when he wasn't around. He used to write the words that he couldn't tell me in my presence.

---

22. *Sofreh* is a cloth or polymer piece spread on the ground or table when having a meal.

Seeing him made me so happy. I wished to be with him forever. I did not notice how tired he was and forgot to make him a cup of tea. "Would you like me to make some tea?" he asked.

"No, I don't want to drink tea now," I said.

"But I will drink."

"Leave it, have it another time."

"Shall we make some together?"

We lit up the stove and scrambled two eggs, then waited until the New Year rang in.

My mom called me, "Don't you want to say Happy New Year to your mom?" she asked. While Manouchehr was next to me, I replied, "Mom, I was tired and cranky, you are with your husband and you feel fine!" Then he took the phone and greeted my mom. The next morning everybody came to our house. We were invited to my father-in-law's house. After that, we borrowed his car and went shopping for New Year's Eve to Vali-Asr Street.[23]

---

23. Vali Asr is the longest treed street in Tehran and the Middle East, which is eighteen kilometers long. There are many shopping centers, public parks, restaurants, museums, cultural centers, and national and international offices on this street.

Fereshteh thought that jeans suited Manouchehr. She took a glance at him from head to toe and said, "Happy new pants." She bought him jeans as a New Year's present, but Manouchehr felt uneasy in those jeans. "Fereshteh, I can't stand these jeans," he said. What a difference! Manouchehr didn't like to wear perfumes and jeans. However, she used to aromatize his clothes secretly. He didn't like to shave his face. His beard was trimmed all the time, but he didn't like to shave it with a razor. Manouchehr didn't put on the gold ring given by her father;[24] He didn't even wear a tie in his wedding party, but Fereshteh liked all those things.

"I feel pity for Manouchehr because he is stuck with you," mother said, and the uncle confirmed her words. Fereshteh was tickled pink because Manouchehr was popular amongst her family. But she frowned and showed evil eyes to Manouchehr and said, "You have no idea when he pesters me."

---

24. According to Islamic law men are not allowed to wear gold.

Chapter 3

You Are in My Heart

I told them all that we would go on a trip during the first week of the New Year. I even unplugged the telephone. We were home alone by ourselves, far from everyone. After the New Year's holidays, Manouchehr enrolled in Sepah[25] and became an official member. During that time, I was feeling dejected and stressed because of my final exams. I thought that I had caught a cold.

---

25. Islamic Revolutionary Guard Corps, or Sepah, is a military and cultural organization, which was established about three months after the victory of the Islamic Revolution of Iran (in April 1979) under Imam Khomeini's advisement to protect the revolution and its achievements and to cooperate with the army of the Islamic Republic of Iran.

I had pain in my bones. Finally, I finished my exams. After work, Manouchehr had gone to my parents' house and had brought *ghormeh sabzi*[26] which mom had cooked for me. Whilst preparing the table for lunch, he looked at me and laughed. "What's wrong? Why do you laugh? I hope you get sick too!" I exclaimed.

"This one is not coming to me!" he said.

"Do you think you are God's gift to mankind?"

"Anyway, I'm happy because I'm going to be a dad and you, a mom!" I couldn't figure out his words. "I'm certain. I've already made a doctor's appointment for you," he said.

He had consulted a doctor, and the doctor had told him that apparently, I was pregnant. Hearing that made me burst into tears, since I wasn't happy with that news. I thought this would strain our relationship. "I went to a doctor for your sake, not the child," he said, and added, "I say this because I just dreamt about it."

In the afternoon, we went to take a test. Then, he went to get the results, but I didn't

---

26. *Ghormeh sabzi* is a traditional popular herb stew, which is often served with rice.

go with him and waited outside. While he was going down the stairs, he was over the moon; It made me doubly jealous and upset. I wanted him just for myself. "Here you are Mom! congratulations!" he said, excitedly while giving me the result.

I was totally fretful. "Don't you want to be a mother?" he asked.

I couldn't stand it anymore and said, "No, I don't want anything to separate us, nothing, even a child. You are on top of the world even before it is born."

He became serious, "Nobody can take you away, you are the apple of my eyes forever," he said reassuringly.

I really couldn't stand anybody between us. I still feel like I did before. If somebody said they loved Manouchehr more, I would get upset. As my children grew older, they came to know this as well. Ali says, "We should do our best to be like dad in our mom's heart." I say, "No, everyone has their own place in my heart."

Ali was born on the birthday of Prophet Muhammad (s). I prayed to have a thin-framed kid, because I liked to feel his bones with my hands. When I hugged him, I had no feeling. I played with his fingers, touched his skin, and his eyes, but I couldn't believe that it was my child. I put my hand on his mouth; he wanted to lick it. At that moment, I perceived what a mother's love meant. I kissed his hands.

> *Manouchehr entered the room with a bunch of dahlia flowers in his hands. His eyes were red and bloodshot because he had cried bitter tears. As soon as he saw Fereshteh, he started to cry, "I didn't expect to see you again." He hugged Ali and kissed his eyes. Ali was just the same as he had seen in his dreams: a boy with big black eyes and long eyelashes. He handed Ali to her and laid some papers on the ground to pray. He hugged Ali again and recited adhan and iqama into his ears.[27] Then he held Ali in his hands and looked at him carefully and said to Fereshteh, "His eyes look like yours; they stare at my eyes and make me surrender." He*

---

27. *Adhan* is a call for Muslims, which informs them of the time of prayer. It is often cast or recited through minarets of mosques. It is recommended in Islam to recite *adhan* into the right ear and *iqama* into the left ear of the baby.

stayed up late the entire night next to Fereshteh's bed. He hadn't slept a wink for a couple of days.

Two weeks later, Manouchehr decided to go to the battlefield, but I did not tell him anything. I never told him whether or not he should go. Ali was a fourteen-day-old infant. I was tired. Manouchehr was praying and crying over and over. "O God, what should I do? It is really cowardly that my friends step on landmines, whilst I'm here with my family having a joyful time. Why do you deprive me of the pleasure of going to the battlefield?" he cried. Military operations were about to begin. Imam Khomeini had stated that Khorramshahr[28] had to be liberated. Manouchehr was calm when I got up. "Have I ever hindered you?" I asked him. "No," he replied. "You want to go? Go then. We have agreed never to stop each other," I said. "You are not feeling well," he said. "Don't worry about me," I reassured him.

---

28. Khorramshahr is a large city in Khuzestan province, southwestern Iran. During the Iraqi war on Iran, the city was occupied by Ba'athi forces for nearly two years, and more than one thousand of its Arab and non-Arab people were killed by the Iraqi army. In 1982, the city was liberated in Operation Beit-ol-Moqaddas.

The following day, he went to the Hazrat Rasool brigade, which was newly formed. He was recruited as an RPG shooter and the head of supplies of the Habib battalion.

She was worried about him because many soldiers were martyred, and there were plenty of operations too. She stroked Manouchehr's photo on the wall affectionately, because she liked it very much. She used to trim his beard herself. Once she shaved his beard up until his chin mischievously, so Manouchehr had no choice but to shave his beard completely.[29] She took that photo, despite Manouchehr's indignation. He had to take a month's leave and stay with Fereshteh. He was embarrassed to go to his workplace with that appearance. But such tricks were not working anymore. She couldn't keep him near herself. Suddenly she got worried for him. She prayed to God to keep Manouchehr safe. She wanted to live with him forever. She prayed for his well-being at the price of everything.

---

29. According to Islamic Shariah it is not permissible for men to shave their beard.

That day he was injured by shrapnel shells. He was taken to Shiraz[30] and then to Tehran. While I was at Manouchehr's aunt's house, he called me. "Where are you? Your voice seems nearby! It's like you are close to me!" I said to him.

"I'm always with you and near you."

"Are you at home?"

"I can't hide anything from you!"

He had gone to my father's house, so I hung up and picked Ali up and went there.

Manouchehr was sitting on the marble stairs near the garden and was smoking. He was pale. He put the cigarette on the corner of his lips and hugged Ali with his right arm. I sat next to him, took the cigarette, and threw it on the pool's edge. As soon as we started to talk, my father and my uncle, with Manouchehr's parents, came into the yard and surrounded him. My uncle hugged him and patted him on his arm, but suddenly Manouchehr went pale, became weak, and sat down. We all got worried for him and helped him inside. His wounded

---

30. Shiraz is one of the biggest and oldest cities in Iran located in the southwestern part of the country in Fars province.

arm was bleeding, and his sleeve was soaked with blood. I knew that he didn't want to let anybody know about it. I put his coat on his shoulders, and we left for the hospital. His shoulder was shell-shocked, and he wasn't able to move his hand. "We need two strong men to hold you, he needs some injections administered in his shoulder," the doctor said. "Nobody should stay here but Fereshteh," Manouchehr said. He took off his shirt and asked the doctor to inject the medicine. I held his hands. While the doctor was injecting, we were gazing into each other's eyes. Seeing his pain and torture was really painful for me. He didn't utter a thing, but he was sweaty. The doctor finished injecting. "What a tight-lipped man you are! Say a word to make me relieved; you really didn't feel the pain?" the doctor asked. "Of course, it was like a torture chamber, but without any confession," Manouchehr replied. The doctor bandaged his arm, and we returned home. He stayed at home for a dozen days with us.

From the kitchen, she craned her neck to see what Manouchehr was doing. He was watching TV, and there was an open book on his legs. Ali was hanging onto his neck, but he paid no

attention to him. He was down in the dumps; he didn't even want to hug Ali. He sounded very distant. He pretended to mind his own business. Ali was ready to take his first steps and liked to grip one's hand to walk. When Manouchehr let go of his hands, he fell down. During the nights, Manouchehr used to turn the light off and recite the Holy Quran with a torch until morning. She was upset. She didn't expect this behavior. They used to go to the cemetery on Thursdays. Once, Manouchehr was going to leave her behind. He had forgotten that she was with him!

The next time that he went to the battlefield, I wrote a detailed letter including all the things that I wanted to say. Having received the letter, he called me and apologized.

I wrote to him the following: "*You give me the cold shoulder, your love is not as warm as before; perhaps you have found a better one.*"

He replied: "*Fereshteh; nobody is better than you for me in this world, but I want to elevate this love to Divine love. I can't. It is hard for me. Here, my friends lie down on the barbed wires and step on mines. But for me, when I want to shoot an RPG, I remember you and Ali*".

I wrote back: "*Yes, you want us to get out of your path.*"

Every time he left, Ali would get a fever, so I had to play with him all night to calm him down. "I understand. You don't want to depend on me. But now you are here, so let's enjoy these moments. We know nothing about the future. The path you have chosen is not an easy one. Let's not feel sorry for these moments later. If you get hurt, Ali's feelings would get hurt; let's make good memories," I told him.

After that, he changed a lot and became like his usual self. I was hand in glove with him. He had fun and played with Ali. He began to mess around with us. He liked to put Ali in the stroller and take a walk. He didn't even let me push the stroller.

> *She put the slices of sangak[31] on the table for breakfast. Manouchehr was at home. She liked to prepare whatever he liked. She heard Ali's giggling from*

---

31. *Sangak* bread is a traditional delicious Iranian bread, which is baked on hot stones in an oven.

the room. She opened the door and found Manouchehr playing with Ali. He lied down on the floor and held Ali in the air. He tickled Ali and burst out laughing. He was his usual self again which pleased her.

His body was full of shrapnel shells, but we couldn't do anything, because they were lodged in his vital organs. From the x-ray images, you could understand that the inside of his body was torn up. I envied the shrapnel shells which were next to his heart, but he told me, "Sweetie, you are in my heart!"

I didn't want to be away from him anymore, particularly when I came to realize that most of the Sepah members' families lived close enough to them, in the south of Iran. On a journey to the vicinity of the battlefield together, with the families of the armed forces, I met Mrs. Karimi, Rabbani, and *haj* Ebadian. They lived in the south. I couldn't stay in Tehran anymore. I was fed up with the separation. Manouchehr had returned to Tehran on a mission for a couple of days. "You should take us with you," I said to him, and he promised to rent a house in the south of Iran and move us there.

While I was packing our belongings, he called and said that he had rented a two-story apartment in Dezful.[32] One of the members of the brigade, Mr. Mousavi, and his wife wanted to live with us. I didn't let anybody know until the departure, because nobody was content with us leaving. "All over the world, when a war begins, people move to safer places, but you want to go to a war zone under bombardment!?" they said. I listened to all of their words. After hearing them, I said, "You have spoken your piece, yes? But everybody chooses their own path in life, and I have chosen my husband."

My parents cried a lot, especially my father. "I can't take you to Dezful with your current situation. If something goes wrong, what am I supposed to do? You should convince them to agree with you," Manouchehr said. So, I had to talk to my father, "Manouchehr is worried about you.

---

32. Dezful is a city in southwestern Iran in Khuzestan Province. During the Iraqi war on Iran, the city came under 160 missile attacks, and nearly 2600 people in the city were martyred. Despite heavy missile attacks, people of Dezful resisted against the Ba'ath occupation.

If he doesn't take us along with him and becomes a martyr, won't you feel sorry for not letting me go with him?" My father hugged Ali, "Would you like to go with your father?" he asked him. "Yes, I miss my daddy," Ali replied. My father showered Ali with kisses, "Take care of yourself, and know that we are really worried about you, although we have to bear it." The next day we left Tehran early in the morning.

Chapter 4

Our Short-lived Life in Dezful

On the pretext of a mission, Manouchehr had left them hanging again. After a couple of days, Mr. Mousavi and his wife left for Tehran. She was alone with Ali in a strange city. They knew no one there. She had thought that the separation was over, and if seeing Manouchehr was not possible every day, she would see him once or twice a week at least!

The city was quiet, and all the inhabitants had left. Manouchehr had left home for almost a month. We were at home in the living room when we heard a noise from the yard. I heard footsteps treading upstairs, and then I saw some men in the yard; I put Ali in his room and locked the door. I called one of Manouchehr's friends and told him what was happening. I always had a gun at home. I grabbed it. As soon as I entered the living room, they saw me and said, "Madam, are you there? Open the door."

"Who are you?" I asked.

"I'm the landlord," one of them said.

"So what? How dare you come in?"

"I found the home vacant, so I've come to see what is going on," he said. They wanted to break in, so I targeted the gun towards them and said, "I will kill you, if any of you try to get inside."

Soon after, two squads of army soldiers arrived and arrested all five of them. The news had reached Manouchehr, and before getting home, he had gone to give the landlord a scolding. Manouchehr had told him, "We all abandoned our city and brought our families to this dire situation, and now, you have taken your family to a safer place and serve us in this way?"

While we were having dinner, somebody knocked on the door. On the intercom, I asked them who they were. "Please open the door," they replied. "Who is it?" I asked again. "Who are you?!" Manouchehr was messing with me. I filled a bucket with water and went up the stairs. I asked him again from the window, "Who are you?" When he raised his head to look at me, I poured the water on his head and ran back down the stairs. He was soaked. "Go back to the place where you were for the last month," I said. "Open the door, please. I beg you!" he said.

I wanted to see him from the bottom of my heart. I opened the door, and he came in. I dried his hair with a towel and told him the story and the events that happened after our neighbor's departure. He was so frightened that he decided to come home twice a week and, if not possible, to make a phone call to us.

Perhaps that event was God's blessing. She didn't lose anything; rather, she had Manouchehr at home again. When Manouchehr was home, everything was great for her.

She thought to herself, how could she characterize Manouchehr? If one asked his friends about Manouchehr, they would say that he was angry and serious. But his grandmother used to say, "Manouchehr's humor crosses the line," as he liked tickling his grandmother.

> *His grandmother used to tell him, "Aren't you a pasdar?[33] Why are you so naughty? pasdars are dignified." His grandmother hadn't seen Manouchehr's charisma. Fereshteh wondered how he could be so mad and yet keep calm and be quiet. She had heard that Husayni sayyids[34] are quick tempered, but Manouchehr was not like that.*

Manouchehr's grandfather was a Husayni *sayyid*. He lived in Baku years ago. His father and his uncles were born there. Although they were all wealthy, people would pay donations to them out of affection. When they moved to Iran, the payments continued. His grandfather felt insulted and sold his genealogy. He even hid that he was a *sayyid* when he obtained an identity booklet. Manouchehr was content with his grandfather's decision. "There are many things which must be proven by the heart, not by words," he said.

---

33. *Pasdar* is a title given to a person who serves in the Islamic Revolutionary Guard Corps, who has the duty of guarding and protecting the values of the Islamic Revolution.
34. Husayni sadaat are people whose lineage goes back to Imam al-Husayn (a), the third Shiite Imam.

In my view, Manouchehr was a true believer in God and a real *sayyid*, as I was witnessing his cautiousness in using public properties. He never used governmental properties for personal affairs. Whenever possible, he didn't receive his ration. He used to wear khaki clothes and Kurdish pants. Once in Dezful, I sewed Ali a pair of pants, using one of Manouchehr's old military pants. When he saw them, Manouchehr got happy, but when he found out that they were made of his old pants, he got angry. I hadn't seen him like that before. "They are not mine, and they belong to the public wealth. Why have you misused them?" he said. "They were yours," I said. "We are involved in a war, and we need them. I could have used them more. We should have enough consideration," he added.

His clothes were worn out. He used to keep the buttons of his torn clothes since he believed they would come in handy one day. He always told me not to waste anything. He asked me to give our leftovers to the birds. In order to give clean food to them, he had made an oil container full of holes; I always put leftovers in that container for the birds.

We were not alone in Dezful anymore, because Mr. Pazuki and his wife moved in upstairs. Mr. Salehi, who was a newlywed, came to Dezful too. Other friends such as Mr. Nami, Karimi, Maleki, *haj* Ebadian, Rabbani, and Torabian brought their families there as well. Two families had rented one flat together. When the men were away from home, the women used to gather together and hang out. Some families lived in Andimeshk.[35] They joined us later. Once I asked Ali, "How many aunts do you have?" He replied, "An Army!" I asked him, "How many uncles do you have?" He replied, "An Army!"

In Operation Badr, the government of Iraq threatened that Dezful would come under bombardment, and they followed through with the threat. The majority of local inhabitants left the city. They wanted to return a couple of days after the bombardment. Some men wanted to take their families away, but everybody stayed and remained there. "You all can come to my house in Andimeshk," Mr. Dastvareh said. However, I didn't go and told Manouchehr

---

35. Andimeshk is a city in south of Iran.

about my decision. I believed I was a strong person and could tolerate it until the end. Even though they insisted, I didn't go. Ali had a painful wart on his foot and he was not able to walk. I took him to the hospital. Due to the bombardment, all the windows were broken. "What do you want me to do in this situation? Go back home!" the doctor said. We returned home. The waves of the bomb blast had flung open the doors. Nobody was there. We had nothing to eat and drink. The water was muddy, and we had no electricity or a phone. While I was sitting by the entrance, I saw a military car that belonged to Sepah. I waved to the car, and it stopped. I asked them to tell Mr. Salehi to bring us some food and water. Mr. Salehi was in charge of the revolutionary guards forces' families. Whatever we were in need of, we would ask him to bring for us. A few hours later, he came and took us to Mr. Dastvareh's home.

> *She had gone to a hospital with some women to help the wounded. When she was informed about Manouchehr's arrival, she rushed to the yard because she missed him a lot. He was standing near the garden of the hospital. When he saw her, he burst into tears, "You don't*

> *know how I was feeling. I thought you were buried under the debris because of the bombardment. I had butterflies in my stomach," he said. She hugged him, "Then, you would be the husband of a martyred woman," but he was still crying with his puffy eyes.*

Manouchehr was informed that the city of Dezful had been bombarded, specifically Taleghani Street, where we lived. He went to Ahvaz and called my mother. She said that somebody had called her and said something vague about Fereshteh and Ali. She thought something terrible had happened. The day we went to Andimeshk, *haj* Ebadian jotted down our home phone numbers and promised to inform our relatives. He had told my mom that everything was fine, but she surmised that something wrong had happened, and they wanted to inform her indirectly. Manouchehr was so frightened that he had to go to Dezful. When he arrived there, he could not even find the house because he had wept so much and his eyes were puffy. His friends met him and told him that his family was in the city of Andimeshk.

Later, we called my mom to inform her we were safe and that everything was fine.

Then, we walked around the city, and he gave me a ride to Shaheed Kalantari Street. As I wanted to get out of the car, he said, "I don't want you to stay here; you must go back to Tehran." However, I had just gotten him back. "If you stay here and get hurt, I will go to the battlefield to die; not for the sake of God anymore. Fereshteh, please go home for my sake!" That night I had a talk with Mrs. Ebadian. We were about thirty families who had gathered in Mr. Dastvareh's home. Sometimes some of us went to Mr. Mamaghani's or Mr. Askari's house, but it was difficult. The women had brainstormed and agreed to return to their cities. The next morning, Mr. Salehi had brought breakfast for us. We asked him to get us train tickets so that we could return home.

> *She had to say goodbye; she didn't have much time. However, she kept silent. She could not express her feelings. She didn't want to leave him, so she stared into his eyes. When she wanted to do something against Manouchehr's consent, she used to stare into his eyes to please him. But at that moment, she couldn't, and she didn't want to persuade him to agree. She said, "Try not to get martyred; I'm not ready for that.*

Be sure; if I don't want it, you can't get martyred!"

"I'm sure! When a mortar falls onto my head and cuts my hair, but it doesn't go off, I attribute that to you. You won't let me go. You won't. I know!" Manouchehr said. Fereshteh breathed deeply. While laughing, she raised her finger toward his face and said, "Watch out and be alert, my dear Manouchehr. I love you too much to make such a deal with God!"

Chapter 5

The Best of Deeds

He embraced Ali and seated him on his knees, "When I'm away, you have to head the family. When you go out, take care of your mom," he said. Since then, whenever I wanted to go out, Ali asked me where I was going and wanted to accompany me. He had a high sense of duty. "Wait. I must escort you!"

Haj Ebadian called Manouchehr and Rabbani, and they left together. It was a very gloomy night. The crickets were singing as if they were sad too. We had learned the way of being in love, but we couldn't enjoy it. The moments when we were sitting next to each other, our minds were obsessed with other things. Men were busy, and women were worried. Women always thought that perhaps this was the last time they would see their men. We never could get enough of each other.

Going to Tehran presented its own problems. We had moved all of our belongings to Dezful. We had no home, so we had to live in my father's house. We used to listen to the news on the radio. In the next military operation, Abbas Karimi and Maleki were martyred; Torabian was injured, and Nami's arm was severed. Mr. Salehi informed us about it. Manouchehr hadn't called me, so I had to ask his friends regarding his health condition.

He called me on New Year's Eve. My voice was trembling on the phone. "Such behavior of yours slackens my soul," he said. I was gloomy. We cried a lot because of those two martyrs. He promised to rent a house and take us there.

> *The exhausted soldier was walking alone with a backpack on his shoulder. She felt that Manouchehr was close! Maybe he had come, so she headed toward Manouchehr's father's house and opened the door. His boots were not there. She went upstairs. There wasn't*

anybody in the room, but she could smell Manouchehr's scent. She thought maybe he wanted to surprise her. When she went to draw the curtains, a bouquet popped up. It was the same kind of bouquet that Manochehr used to buy for her back in the day; there were many different kinds of flowers. She was pleased that she trusted her heart and went there.

I forgave his three-month absence, because he had fulfilled his promise. He had rented a house together with Mr. Esfandiari in the city of Shush.[36] There were two rooms in our house there. One of them was bigger and brighter than the other. Manouchehr had arranged our furniture in the smaller room. "They have just gotten married; his wife is new around here. I think she may feel homesick, that's why I put our things here. Now, I will do whatever you say!" he said. I agreed. He brought some empty boxes of munitions to be used as closets, two of them for us and the rest for them. The next day, Mr. Esfandiari and his wife

---

36. Shush is an ancient city in Iran, located in the southwestern part of the country in Khuzestan province.

moved their furniture into the house. And Manouchehr left me again as soon as he was sure that I was not alone! After some days, Mr. Esfandiari left us too.

We were just three people at home, and we had to busy ourselves with many things. We used to go to the mosque, *basij*, or the shrine of Prophet Daniel.[37] Sometimes we would watch TV at home. In Dezful, we could watch Iraqi channels better than Iranian channels. I would climb up an old ladder to go to the roof and set the antenna. One of the channels was showing the war captives for propaganda purposes. Some of the prisoners were introducing themselves and giving their addresses and phone numbers. We jotted down their names and phone numbers and then called their families to inform them about their soldiers. To put it differently, together, we had founded a committee for the captives! But we didn't have a telephone line. So, we had to go to the telecommunications office to make phone calls. Sometimes, I asked my

---

37. Prophet Daniel (Daniyal Nabi) was an Israelite prophet who was imprisoned by the Assyrian king, together with several other Israelites. He passed away in Shush, where he was buried.

mom to call them. We did all these things when our husbands were on the battlefield. But when they came back, we used to go to the shrine and pray up until midnight. We knew that if they went away, we wouldn't see them for a week.

My mom, along with my brothers and sisters, traveled to Shush to visit me and stayed for some days. Mr. Esfandiari informed me of this in advance. For a moment, I thought that they were coming to take me back to Tehran, so I became weak. Mr. Esfandiari immediately called a doctor to visit me. The doctor told me I was pregnant. As soon as Manouchehr was informed, he came home immediately. On the way home, he had picked some flowers for me. That night, he stayed home with me. He didn't let me do anything, and I didn't lift a finger. Every half an hour, he went out to buy different things for me. He even bought a new lemon-colored dress for the new baby, because he was sure about the gender of our child. Manouchehr knew the gender of both of our children before their birth! A day later, he said he couldn't stay home and wanted to go to the shrine. He wanted to be alone and get something off his chest. My mother came to me with Fahimeh, Mohsen, and Fariborz.

After some days, Manouchehr sent me back to Tehran with my family, because the armed forces were supposed to move to the west. He wasn't able to visit us for two months. But I couldn't stand it, and after two months, I returned to Dezful in the south. However, I didn't stay there for a long time, because I wasn't feeling well. The doctor ordered me to go back to Tehran, so I had to pack my belongings and return to Tehran again.

She craved watermelon. There was a pick-up truck ahead of them, which was carrying watermelons. She whispered to Manouchehr -while he was driving- that she wanted it. He sped up and, while driving, asked the van driver to stop! But those watermelons were not for sale. The driver was just delivering them to another place. Manouchehr insisted a lot and eventually bought one of them. "Wow! Shall we wait until we get home? Let's eat it right away!" Fereshteh exclaimed. But they didn't have a knife. Manouchehr took two screwdrivers from the trunk, washed them, and used them to cut the watermelon into pieces. He nodded his head and said, "What a pampered girl I'm going to have, she wants the world!"

Actually, Hoda is not the kind of girl who wants everything. She is patient and reserved, like her father. She is an image of her father in behavior and appearance. She was born in April 1986. That day, Manouchehr was over the moon. Everyone in the hospital thought that we had been married for fifteen years, but hadn't had any children up until then! He bought two large boxes of confectionery and served it to everybody in the hospital. Furthermore, he brought a giant bouquet of red clover, which passed through the door with difficulty.

Hoda was a brunette and chubby girl. Manouchehr used to shower her with kisses. When he was home, he liked to wrestle with Ali and play with Hoda. Moreover, he liked to buy toys for them. Hoda had a closet full of toys! He used to say, "I can't resist! Maybe it will be hard for me when I'm away and not able to see you. But I'm happy that I have hugged them, kissed them, and played with them abundantly."

He never struggled with the kids. He always told me not to hit them, because the children wouldn't forget about it. He treated them as adults. When he wanted to feed them, he would ask them whether they liked to eat or not. He was patient and liked to feed them chunk by chunk.

After Hoda's birth, we didn't go to the war zone. That year, Ali started school. During Operation Karbala-5,[38] *haj*[39] Ebadian was martyred. He was Manouchehr's best friend. Since then, Manouchehr became gloomy. If you asked him which day was the hardest day of his life, he would have said, "The day that *haj* Ebadian was martyred." After his martyrdom, Manouchehr felt very unhappy and despondent. He used to walk, cry and sigh a lot. He didn't want to go to the war zone and see *haj* Ebadian's vacant seat. Manouchehr ached for him a lot. During that operation, Manouchehr got injured in a chemical attack. His skin was blistered, and his eyes were watery. But because it was concurrent with his cries, I couldn't figure out if it was from his crises or from the tears that welled up in his eyes as a result of his friend's martyrdom.

Consecutive martyrdoms, my solicitude to my husband and worry for him, and the

---

38. Operation Karbala-5 is an operation carried out by Armed Forces of Iran during the Iraqi war on Iran to conquer Basra. It was the most costly and the deadliest Iranian operation during the Iraqi war on Iran.
39. *Haj* or *haji* is a person who has performed the *hajj* ritual. The title is often used before a person's name. In the Iranian culture, the term is also used to address a man respectfully.

bombardment of Tehran saddened me; I didn't feel like doing anything. I even lacked my usual appetite, and I was extremely irritable. Manouchehr was not at home. I called him and told him that I was scared. He replied, "There is a war within me too. Do you think I am not afraid of that?" I couldn't believe that he feared at all. He was a hero in my mind! He said, "I like my life with you, as much as I yearn for martyrdom, but I have to choose one over the other. Ultimately, we should surrender our hearts to God." His words made me calm, and I decided to leave my parents and return to my home after a while.

A couple of days later, he called me, "Fereshteh, go and look around the bombarded areas with the kids," he said. I wondered why. He said, "To see how selfish human beings can be." I didn't want to talk to him, not because I was bothered, but because I was embarrassed. We went to the recently bombarded areas. Some people were sitting on piles of soil, a kid was calling her mother, who was buried under the debris. But just some steps away, some others were buying goldfish[40] for the New Year, as if there was

---

40. Nowruz goldfish is a small red-colored fish used by Iranians in celebration of the new solar year as a

nothing to worry about. I really didn't want to be like them, neither steeped with my happiness, nor my sadness, because both of them account for selfishness. Manouchehr wanted me to realize these facts. He always gave me encouragement to know myself better.

In 1988 Manouchehr became in charge of the Belal Garrison in Karaj.[41] From that moment on, he came home more often. When he was not away for a mission, he used to go to work in the morning and return in the evening.

> *She looked at him. He had rolled up his sleeves and was ready to perform wudhu.[42] She had grown accustomed to him more and more. She used to get worked up when he wanted to go to the war zone as if she had no more patience. Fereshteh wanted Manouchehr to lead*

---

decoration of their Haftsin cloth. The tradition dates back to the pre-Islamic era.

41. Karaj is the capital of Alborz Province.

42. *Wudhu* is a ritual ablution of one's face and hands, and wiping one's head and feet in a particular manner. In Islam, *wudhu* is required for the validity of the prayer and some other acts of worship.

her in prayer, but Manouchehr was too humble to do such a thing. Once, he became aware that Fereshteh had followed him in prayer and became upset. After that, he would find a corner of the house where it was impossible to pray behind him and would pray there. One time he had his eyes closed and was reciting the call to prayer (adhan). When he had reached "Come to the best of deeds,"[43] Fereshteh suddenly jumped towards him and started kissing him. Manouchehr stopped, turned his head towards her, and said, "My dear! Why do you do such things? When I go towards the best of deeds, you come and do wicked things." Fereshteh ruffled some of his wet hair and replied, "In my book, this is the best of deeds."

Maybe life was easier during the first six months of our marriage, but after 1988, I couldn't bite the bullet anymore. I used to be more dependent on him. I wished every day to be Friday[44] because he stayed at home

---

43. "Come to the best of deeds" is one of the phrases of *adhan*.
44. Friday is a holiday of the week according to the Iranian calendar.

on Fridays.

Chapter 6

A Victim of Chemical Weapons

After the war, he sometimes went to the war zones to control and clean the borders. He was losing weight; he could not eat food because it hurt his stomach. Every kind of food seemed spicy to him. Nobody knew exactly about the chemical weapons that were used and their side effects. Even the doctors couldn't recognize them. Every time he was referred to the hospital, medics prescribed him a serum and admitted him to rest for two days; then, we returned home.

There was a high financial pressure during those years. Manouchehr bought a car and started to make money with that in the evenings, but traffic and noise annoyed him. He couldn't continue with that.

His cousin, Nader, had an old-fashioned restaurant in Naser Khosrow.[45] After work at the garrison, he used to go there to sell milk in the evenings. I didn't know about it. When I got to know, I became angry and asked him the reason. "I'm sick of this situation; I'm overwhelmed with shame," he replied. "Are you disturbed?" I asked. "No. I work because I'm concerned with my family's well-being," he replied.

Later, he enrolled in a school and continued his studies again. He was supposed to cover the courses of a year in just three months. He was good at everything except dictation.

She opened the book of Farsi literature and dictated some texts to him. He had awful handwriting. She used to say, "You have such bad handwriting that your teachers won't be able to grade your papers," and he replied, "They will learn how to mark my papers." Fereshteh had learned how to read his style of writing because of his

---

45. Naser Khosrow Street is a historic downtown street in Tehran.

unique handwriting. She counted his errors and said, "You have made sixty-eight errors! You have failed!" While turning the papers over, he replied, "I will study to pass it." She was sure that he could do it. He was so firm and stubborn that he achieved whatever he set out to do.

He used to go to the park to study his books from 4:30 to 7 a.m. and then go to the garrison. After office hours, he used to go to Nader's restaurant, again with his books! He was using every moment to study. He aced his dictation test. He really enjoyed studying. Due to his migraine, medics discouraged him from studying so much, so he left school at the beginning of the ninth grade. Because of shrapnel shells in his head, his nose and ear would constantly bleed. Doctors had warned him to avoid stress. Some of his friends had promised to provide him with a fake high school diploma and even a university acceptance, but he didn't accept them. Rather he got annoyed. "I want to learn; I should have enough knowledge to attend university. What is the use of a fake certificate?" he would argue.

After the war and Imam Khomeini's demise, the lives of those involved in the war changed drastically. We were forgotten; it was as if everyone forgot about us and we also became disconnected from them. We were not ready for a life post-war, as many things had changed. Once, Manouchehr said, "I need to make an appointment at the office of the person who used to be a close friend of mine! I have to get permission from his secretary!"

During those times, there was a concern over ranking based on education, the severity of wounds[46] made in the war, and the duration of presence in the war. Manouchehr didn't present any evidence proving his presence in the war. He tended to keep it to himself, but sometimes he grew impatient. He even resigned, but his resignation was rejected. In 1990, he went to the war zone for four months, but his

---

46. The severity of wounds or veteran disability rating (in Persian, darsad janbazi) is the extent of physical and psychological disability of veterans. In Iran, the Organization of Martyrs and Veterans Affairs provides veterans with facilities and advantages based on the rating of their disability.

health worsened there, and once again, he vomited blood. He was taken to a hospital in Tehran. His body, from head to toe, was examined with x-rays, but the doctors couldn't diagnose the problem. After a week, he returned home. "Fereshteh, I have an upset stomach; I feel that my stomach is swelling," he said. Jamshid had brought some fresh berries. When he ate them, he couldn't breathe, so we took him to the hospital immediately. His intestines were obstructed. The doctors performed a biopsy on his intestines, and I took it to a laboratory. They had taken him to the operating room before I could even arrive. While walking up the stairs, a medical student stopped me, "Mrs. Mudeq, the doctors have diagnosed his illness as cancer, but can't find the exact place of tumor, so they are going to cut his abdomen and locate it," they said. "I won't let them do that," I said. They had prepared Manouchehr for the operation room. "If you touch him, I will make you pay for it," I said. I found a piece of cotton saturated in alcohol and separated his serum. Then I dressed him and called my father to come to the hospital and pick us up. I wanted to take him out of the hospital, but due to my insistence, the doctor wrote a letter and introduced us to Dr. Mir, who was a tumor surgeon in Jam hospital. Manouchehr was confined to a bed in the hospital on the Day of Ashura.[47]

Although he had a serum attached to him, the moment he heard the *adhan*, he stood up and performed his prayers while weeping. While praying, he said to God, "O Lord, I want to complain. I was on the battlefield for some years. Why have you taken me to the hospital? I do not wish for such a death." He then sat on the bed and said to me, "I made a mistake. I blame it on you. Every time that I wanted to go, you came to my mind. Now, leave me alone." I knew that all of his unkindness was to make me abandon him. But I said, "I'm here forever, and I won't leave you alone. You'll

---

47. The Day of Ashura is the tenth of Muharram (the first lunar month in the Hijri calendar). On the Day of Ashura in 61 AH/October 13, 680, Imam al-Husayn (a), the third Shiite Imam, was martyred along with his companions in Karbala by the army of Yazid, the Umayyad caliph, in an unequal war while he was thirsty. The event is a major occurrence in the history of Islam. Every year at the anniversary of the event, the Shias hold mourning ceremonies on the first ten days of Muharram and pledge their allegiance to the goals of Imam al-Husayn (a).

see, my darling." We were able to overcome many tribulations during the war. I surmised that we would pass these difficult days too, and during our old age, we would laugh at these moments!

He didn't have an appetite for the food served in the hospital. The doctor said, "He can eat anything, and it makes no difference." I asked Jamshid to bring some food from the religious ceremonies held for Imam Husayn (a). We fed all of the patients in that ward of the hospital. Two plates of food were left for us. One of the patients came to us and said that he hadn't received any food. Manouchehr gave his food to him and the three of us shared one plate together. I was really worried about him because his intestines were obstructed again. He was fine in the evening. "I'm sure about one thing, Imam Husayn (a) likes me. Whatever happens to me, he will help me, and I will stay silent," he said.

She stayed up the whole night and prayed. She stared at Manouchehr, sleeping calmly as if he had a lot of work to do. She hated herself because she had learned how to pretend, but in fact, she had whimpered a lot when alone. Doctors had diagnosed him with an

advanced kind of intestinal cancer that had infected his stomach. Moreover, they received the report from the Sepah medical commission: he was a disabled war veteran who had incurred ninety percent physical damage to his body. However, they didn't accept whether those injuries occurred during the war. They said that Manouchehr's illness was hereditary; everybody was angry. But he himself laughed and said, "I had these shrapnel shells in my body from the beginning. They are right," but she couldn't keep silent as Manouchehr did.

We were alone before the operation. He took my hand, put it on his chest, and said, "My heart wants you to stay with me forever, but my mind says that you have sacrificed yourself for me since you were fifteen. God created many beauties of life for His creatures; you should enjoy them." His lips were shivering. "I had a lot of good times with you, your return from the battlefield, your existence, and your breathing. I get happy when I see you," I told him. "I haven't been a good husband to you. From now on, I won't be either. You will be ruined," he said. "Let's do this together," I told him comfortingly.

Meanwhile, Jamshid and Rasoul arrived. The nurses came and wanted to take him to the operating room, but he didn't let them. "My feet are still healthy; I want to walk; I'm not paralyzed yet," he told them. He kissed Jamshid and Rasoul in front of the operating room door and then kissed both of my hands twice. "These hands have toiled a lot. From now on, they will have to bear some more," he said. He looked at me and asked whether I would be by his side forever or not. "Yes, I will," I replied. He left without looking at me.

She sat on the edge of Manouchehr's bed in a daze and thought, "What would happen if he never returns?" What would she do? She was out of her mind. She was restlessly waiting for the outcome of the operation. The doctors had no hope and said to Fereshteh, "He needs your blessings."

She performed ablution several times but couldn't concentrate on her prayers. She was all at sea and she didn't know what to do. Finally, she was called upon at noon.

She could hardly walk to the recovery room. There were six beds

> *in the room. Two of the patients were roaring in pain; one was vomiting, the other one was calling a woman's name, and the other two men were clearly in a lot of agony. Manouchehr's bed was on the left corner of the room. She looked at his chest and realized that he was breathing heavily. She then turned and looked at the doctor and waited. The doctor said, "When unconscious, people's souls tend to show themselves. He has a pure soul." She moved closer to Manouchehr and listened to him carefully; he was reciting the adhan.*

He was reciting *dhikr*[48] throughout the time he was unconscious. The doctors had cut a piece of his liver, stomach, and intestine. He was forbidden to have any visitors. His wound was infected, so he couldn't eat anything for two weeks. After that, little by little, he started on a liquid diet.

---

48. Muslims are encouraged to remember God by repeating and reciting phrases such as Subhān Allāh (immaculate is Allah), Allāhu akbar (Allah is the greatest), and Lā ilāaha illā Allāh (There is no deity except Allah). These phrases, which are reminders of God, are called "*dhikr*".

He had to have chemotherapy. The doctors examined his body's marrow and measured the cancer's degree. Dr. Mir introduced Dr. Shafaeiyan, who was a hematologist. On the day of the test, I suffered a lot. I felt pity for him. I wish he would sigh loudly to become calm. His patience and silence made him popular among doctors and nurses. They did their best to help him. Before the results came out, he was dismissed.

The days after his hospitalization were some of the happiest days of my life. I was really happy. I couldn't even stop laughing. Jamshid and I took his arm to help him walk to the elevator, but he said, "I want to walk on my own." Jamshid was standing to his right side, his other brother, Behrooz, was standing to his left side, and I was standing behind Manouchehr to ensure he wouldn't fall. There were three cars to take us home. His family sacrificed a sheep in front of Manouchehr. Ali and Hoda had cleaned the house. They had arranged flowers from the front yard to decorate Manouchehr's bedroom. There was a big vase of flowers on the top of his bed.

Regarding the test reports, the doctor said, "He must start chemotherapy as soon as possible." I was worried about the shortage of medication. I had to go to Naser Khosrow to find some of them. There were long queues of people in front of the Red Crescent office, 13-Aban drugstore, and other professional drugstores.

Manouchehr's friends tried to issue his identity card from the Organization of Disabled Veterans, but it took a long time. We put our house up for sale to buy medicine and had to rent a house. Manouchehr had chemotherapy three times a month. After taking his medication, he said, "I feel hot as if I am in a furnace." Some days he would be nauseous. He also had an ulcer in his mouth and throat, and as a result, he could barely swallow his saliva. He had completely lost his hair due to the chemotherapy.

> *Manouchehr closed his eyes and asked Fereshteh to shave his head and his face with a razor because the remaining hair annoyed him a lot. She tried to talk so much because sometimes talking was hard but being silent was harder. Fereshteh held a mirror in front of him and said, "You look attractive. Look at yourself." Manouchehr touched his face and chin and then laid on the bed while his eyes were closed.*

I compared Manouchehr with his first days. The days he had hair and I would pull on it mischievously, and the days when he didn't even have any eyelashes; it made no difference to me. Manouchehr was living with us, he was breathing, and he was all of my life, and taking care of him had become my whole life, so much so that I forgot to enroll the kids in school. Ali started his first year in middle school, and Hoda started her first year in primary school. I used to sleep near Manouchehr's bed on the floor. One night, I woke up to his voice, saying, *"Ya Husayn"*; he had a dream and had become sweaty. He dreamt that he had lifted the chandelier.[49] "It was very heavy. It felt like all my bones were going to break. I heard them breaking; all of my teeth broke and fell into my mouth," he said. Manouchehr was upset, so he described his dream to one of his friends who was visiting, and he said that Manouchehr had changed his beliefs!

During those days, people reproached and even vilified us since Manouchehr had

---

49. Chandelier or *chilchirāgh* is a symbolic apparatus on which lanterns are installed. *Chilghirāgh* is taken around by Shias as part of the mourning ceremony for Imam al-Husayn (a). The ritual is called "*chilchirāgh-kishī*".

lost his beard due to chemotherapy, and I couldn't wear any *chador* while helping him walk. I couldn't stand his pain. So, I called someone who could interpret dreams. "It means martyrdom, a death with a lot of difficulties," they told me.

We were happy because he was up and about after a while. He used to walk in the afternoons. I had to chase him to ensure he wouldn't fall, although I knew he was sensitive to it. He once said, "I would appreciate your help, as long as I see no pity in your eyes." We didn't let him know that he was having chemotherapy. We told him that he was having some kind of protein therapy. He went to the cinema and watched *From Karkheh to Rhein*.[50] It was from watching this film that Manouchehr became aware

---

50. *From Karkheh to Rheine* is a film written and directed by Ebrahim Hatamikia about the fates of some victims of chemical attacks by the Ba'ath regime on Iran. In this film, an Iranian veteran who was blinded after the Ba'ath regime's chemical attacks, was sent to Germany for treatment along with a number of his comrades. With the efforts of the physicians, the sight of one eye is recovered, but tests show that as a result of the chemicals, he has blood cancer. After an unsuccessful treatment, he becomes a martyr.

of the truth regarding his own condition. Upon returning home, he had a long face. He couldn't believe that I lied to him. He blamed himself and said, "Undoubtedly, I have been acting like a coward."

> *But the fact is that 'cancer means death,' something she didn't want Manouchehr to think about. Manouchehr always envied the martyrs. He had cancer, and Fereshteh didn't want him to pine. Manouchehr described the beauties of death to her and said, "God loves me and has given me a chance to worship and pray more up to the intended day." Fereshteh became drowned in his words. Manouchehr tapped on her leg and said, "Stop with the pessimism! Let's keep walking. Show me who is pushier!"*

My job was to pray to God. I think that my insistence made him come back from the war alive. I thought that he was indestructible, that is, he goes to the point of death and comes back again. Every morning, I breathed easily since another night passed customarily, but I was afraid of the coming night. Due to his bleeding stomach, he would sometimes have high or low blood pressure. We even had to take him to the hospital and receive some blood units. The reason for the bleeding was the presence of a big tumor on his duodenum artery, but the doctors couldn't remove it. While Dr. Shafaeiyan was telling me about it, I wished I could cry and choke to death. The doctor said, "You can cry as much as you want, but you should only smile when you are next to him, as usual! He must be strong enough to fight his illness; maybe, we *might* be able to help him with chemotherapy and radiotherapy." But this "*might*" was a must to me. I saw how Manouchehr was losing weight. His body had swollen because of the Crotone drugs, but after a couple of weeks of radiotherapy, he was as light as a feather, and I could lift him by myself. I didn't want to leave him alone even for a second. I wanted to make use of all the time I had with him. I was afraid of tomorrow; what if he was far from me and needed me to assist him? What if I was unable to see the pain in his eyes to know he needed my help? I didn't want to let him out of my sight at all.

I used to forget all of the difficulties I was going through just by stealing a glance at him. In a circle of friends, he used to say, "A single hair of Fereshteh is more valuable for me than the whole world, and I will wait on her hand and foot." His words reinvigorated me all the time. I wouldn't feel tired because he was standing next to me. Living with Manouchehr never tired me. Sometimes, we would forget our hardships. We were going through very testing times, but we had so much fun and were happy together.

> *She told him a joke, one of those special jokes that she used to say every day, but Manouchehr had a slight frown of disapproval on his face. Then, Fereshteh said, "When you frown, you look weird and funny." Manouchehr burst into laughter and said, "My lady, why do you pick on my tribe? These remarks are unpleasant." She had heard it several times. She wanted to prove that she had learnt her moral lessons well. She said, "a good person…" but she couldn't complete her sentence because it seemed insipid for her. Rather she said, "You are from nowhere! You can't even claim that you are pure Mudeq, because they have injected different blood into you!", and Manouchehr replied, "That may be so, but at least I'm pure Iranian."*

He was very organized and subtle in all affairs, even his sense of humor. He always paid attention to the small things which surprised me. Whenever we went hiking, he would always carry a plastic bag with him to avoid littering. He didn't like to go to the extremities in his affairs, even in his conversations, but on the contrary, I was talkative. I was scared that he might think about something in his loneliness that I was afraid of. I didn't allow him to write a will; I said, "You have made your will with your life and behavior; moreover, you do not possess any wealth!" I had to scrape the bottom of the barrel to deflect his attention from death.

During those days, a group of TV staff came to our home to run a documentary about his memories, but they didn't broadcast that program for a couple of months. They said that it was not ready to air. One night, he called me to watch a TV program about his friend, Madani, who was injured in the war. It displayed his life from hospitalization to martyrdom, and then his funeral. Madani was a disabled war veteran. "I understand. They are waiting for me to pass away," Manouchehr said. He couldn't hold back his tears, and his eyes were filled with tears. Then, he raised his hand and pointed to me, "If they call again, tell them that waiting for someone's death to air a TV program is not a forgivable task," he said.

Fereshteh couldn't forgive them either. It seemed as though everybody was an outsider. She had told Manouchehr over and over to have a word with the media about his current unacceptable situation by going on camera for an interview, but he didn't speak a word. At least, she was expecting the office of war veterans and martyrs to call and greet him on the National Day of Disabled War Veterans. She had waited for them. She washed the stairs and tidied up the house. Then, she prepared everything for the guests and looked forward to them, but nobody came. She didn't let him feel alone. She didn't want him to think that he had been neglected. She didn't want him to say: "I wish I could become a martyr." She didn't want Manouchehr to feel that he was good for nothing or that he was a useless person.

He expressed his sadness with silence and eyes full of tears. However, I considered it my responsibility to complain about and protest against the unacceptable situation of veterans in Sasan Hospital. I wanted to yell at the hospital. I wanted to ask them, "Why do you claim to prioritize veterans, but when it comes to us (veterans), you give us the runaround? Why do you delay our cases?" Manouchehr had to queue in the Baqiyatullah Hospital for a lung scan. As it turned out, his lungs were infected. He was then bedridden for four months. In 1994, Manouchehr began radiotherapy. Until 2000, whenever he wanted to breathe deeply, he used to say that he could smell overcooked meat coming from his stomach. He suffered a lot from all these pains. But he didn't expect a friend to say: "If I were in your shoes, I would have preferred to die instead of being an addict." Manouchehr didn't like to groan; he would be at peace whenever he took some morphine. But these words made me sad, and they were spoken by people who didn't know anything about the war and its difficulties. I wished I could run them over, break their legs, and then see if they could resist taking painkillers and tolerate the pain.

It seemed Manouchehr had a deal with God. He even refused to lose his groans in vain. He would always say, "These pains are signs of courtship with God!" I found my entire life in him, his voice, and his eyes that would wash away the pain within my heart. He used to play pranks on me when I was wrapped up in my thoughts. By saying "Sweetie," he made me forget all about them, and the house would be filled with joy.

We lived in Hakimiyeh residential complex for two years. The military provided us with an apartment. After a while, we sold our car, received a loan from the Organization of War Veterans and Martyrs, and purchased an apartment. The apartment was located in the suburbs, and the vicinity was hilly. Since the air was fresh and clean, Manouchehr could breathe easily and had to use the oxygen tank to a lesser extent. We used to hike in the afternoons. We bought a portable stove and a small pan to make omelets. We used to take a kettle, a small teapot, and a thermos, and then go hiking, just like old times, when we were newly engaged. We also liked going to Qeytarieh Park[51] with Ali and Hoda. He bought a bicycle for them. He liked to hold the handlebar of Hoda's bicycle and walk alongside her to train her in cycling and pedaling. Hakimiyeh County was far from downtown and the hospital, so we were

---

51. Qeytarieh Park is a park in northern Tehran, located in Qeytarieh neighborhood. It has an area of 103000 square meters.

incapable of doing anything in emergency situations. It was frigid during winters, to the extent that the gasoil we kept at home froze. We went through a lot of difficulties, and as a result, we moved to the third floor of my father's house, which was recently renovated. Fariba and Jamshid were living on the second floor. Manouchehr felt like being nearer to the roof of the house. He used to go there most of the time.

> *She grabbed Manouchehr's hands while he was holding binoculars and looking at the sky and said, "I hate the roof of the house because it separates us. Let's go downstairs." Fereshteh couldn't stand that the sight of the sky and some birds had occupied his attention and had kept him on the roof for hours. "I hope to cleave the sky and see higher," Manouchehr said. "There is no binocular capable of that," said Fereshteh. "Of course there is. I should make it with my heart, but my heart is too weak," he said. Fereshteh pulled back her hands and just like children who make excuses, said, "I don't understand you. This place keeps you away from me. Let's leave." He then put the binoculars away, held her wrist, and said, "You can come here if you miss me. I'm just here on the roof."*

Whenever I feel gloomy, I go up to the house's roof. Ever since his departure, I couldn't rest at ease for almost a year. I used to walk unremittingly. I would calm down when I sat on the platform where he always liked to sit, exactly in front of the pigeons' cage. He liked sitting on the roof, stretching his legs, and pouring seeds around himself. Then, birds would come and jump on his legs and begin to eat the seeds. Some of his birds were snowy white, and some others had a patch around their necks. He didn't like black and brown pigeons. I asked him what aspect of them made him interested. "I like their ability to fly," he replied. He wished to feel death but didn't wish to die while sleeping. His friend Saeed, a disabled veteran, had a breathing issue. Once, when his breathing stopped while sleeping, he passed away on the way to the hospital. I noticed that Manouchehr had insomnia for a couple of nights. He didn't want to die unknowingly. So, I had to stay awake until he fell asleep. It wasn't hard for me. Although I had to sleep only for a few hours after the *adhan* in the morning, I wasn't weary.

Manouchehr stayed awake the first night, so we recited supplication of Imam

Ali (a)[52] until morning together, over and over. I used to recite chapter al-Fateha[53] for him to fall asleep on the other nights. I used to put my hand on the part of his body where he had pain and recite al-Fateha seventy times. For a short while, he was steeped with the memories of Dokouheh[54] and his war buddies. He was at a loss.

One night, there was a movie about the war on TV. One of the commanders in the movie, having heard the code, shouted and said, "Go! go and kill them! Destroy them!" Suddenly Manouchehr yelled in a fit of rage and said, "Shame on you and your movies. Which war commander ordered his soldiers to attack and destroy in the war? Was it a conquest? Why do you corrupt everything?"

---

52. Supplication of Imam Ali (a) in the Mosque of Kufa is a mystical supplication by Imam 'Ali (a) in which he talks to God and asks for His mercy.

53. Chapter al-Fateha or al-Hamd is the first chapter of the Quran. When visiting a sick person, It is recommended to recite it and ask for his healing.

54. Dokouheh is an area near Andimeshk in Khuzestan province, which is home to one of the biggest Iranian military bases. During the Iraqi war on Iran, Dokouheh military base was the main operational base in Khuzestan.

He closed his eyes and began to snarl out. He stayed awake all night. The next day in the morning, he left home early. Our house was close to Bagh-e-Feyz, in which there were buried two of the descendants of the Imams. He used to go there and let off steam. On the way home, he had bought *barbari*.[55] His eyes were puffy because he had cried a lot. I greeted him, and he replied, "I'm at the end of the rope. I feel like I want to die." And I said jokingly, "A person whose number is up never buys bread." He gave a short laugh. "You always poke fun at my words," he said. But that day, I couldn't cheer him up. He was moody. He had dreamt about the kids, but he didn't describe his dream.

> *Considering his long prayers, she figured out that he was yearning for his friends. Fereshteh always wanted to be similar to Manouchehr in his way of thinking. She wanted to look at the bright side of everything like Manouchehr did. But how? "If you are honest with God in all of your affairs, if you eat, sleep, laugh, cry or even fall in love for the sake of God,*

---

55. *Barbari* bread is a type of traditional bread in Iran, which has a particular taste and smell.

> *you won't see the dark side of anything, and everything will be fine!" said Manouchehr. Fereshteh found all the beauties of life in Manouchehr. She used to laugh and cry with him. She was repeating this piece of a poem with him:*
>
> *"Human beings take pride in their capabilities, but because of their arrogance, God punishes them. The more arrogance, the more degradation!"*
>
> *Why did he like to repeat this poem? He always minded his own business. He did not have any official position. Fereshteh asked the reason behind it, and he said, "I read it for my heart."*

Actually, I didn't find any caprice or aspiration in him. He was a real square shooter. I remember once he said, "After my death, when you want to bury me in the grave, pour a fist of soil on my face." I asked why, and he replied, "I want to come to this understanding that this world isn't worth sinning for." I asked him, "How sinful are you?" And he replied, "God doesn't like to decry His creatures. I know that I'm sinful."

Later, he got worse day by day. The doctors alleviated him with morphine and painkillers. He was under the weather in January. He couldn't breathe properly. I said to him, "Leave it. Let's not throw Ali a birthday party," but he didn't agree. "We haven't done anything to make our kids happy. They neither go to parties nor go on picnics. The only fun they have is visiting me in the hospital," he said.

He ordered a big cake in the shape of a piano. We invited some of our friends as well.

She was blessed because she had Manouchehr, and she was happy because Ali and Hoda had a father like Manouchehr. The kids' love for their father made Fereshteh happier. Manouchehr had set some rules for New Year's shopping, from the youngest member to the eldest one, first Hoda, then Ali, and finally, Fereshteh and Manouchehr. But Ali, Hoda, and Fereshteh began to buy clothes for Manouchehr unconsciously. Although Manouchehr objected to their decision, they continued. On Mother's Day, Manouchehr received more gifts than Fereshteh. The kids

> *had bought a deodorant spray for Fereshteh and a scarf, gloves, shirt, and a playsuit for Manouchehr. The love of each family member was the best gift for her.*

Chapter 7

White Pigeon

I always say to the kids, "You are very lucky that you saw your father, listened to his words, unburdened yourselves by talking to him, had the chance to ask him your questions, and felt his love. It was worth the difficulties that you went through."

Two days before the New Year in 2000, he felt twinges in his stomach. I guessed that he was going to die. While enduring great pain, he said, "Open the window. I want to jump out of the window to die." He had an ache in his stomach, feet, and chest. As if he was at death's door. I prayed to God to give him another chance. I always wished for people to never lose their loved ones at the turn of the New Year. I didn't want the kids to have sad memories in their minds and rake over the ashes in the future.

I was standing by him, but I had my hands tied, and I could not do anything to help him. I just saw him suffering from pain for a day and a half. I wanted to ask the kids to come to the hospital to celebrate the New Year beside him, but fortunately, the doctors discharged him, and we returned home. I wished I could prostrate to God for hours and thank him. I knew that he would not remain long in this world, therefore, I prayed to God for some more days to help him. I had to choose the lesser of the two evils. He would always comfort me by saying, "Your choice is not between the lesser of two evils. It is between good and better. You have yet to choose the better!"

It seemed as if he was aware that he was no longer for this world, and the year 2000 was his last year of life. We were told beforehand too. We were praying for him. Hoda set the *haftsin*[56] table before the turning of the New

---

56. *Haftsin sofreh* is an annual tradition of the Iranians in Nowruz (the beginning of the solar year). Iranians decorate "tablecloths" with seven things that begin with the Persian letter "س" (sin), each of which is a symbol of a benevolent notion.

Year next to his bed, and we all sat around his bed. He was reciting his prayers on his bed. He used to recite prayers during the last moments of the older year. It was the ending part of his prayers. Hoda, Ali, and I kept an eye on him. The idea that he might pass away made us cry. He looked happy while reciting his prayers. He was full of sobriety and enthusiasm, but we were out of our minds with worry. Having said his prayers, Manouchehr hugged all of us, "You guys are worried about what might happen, whilst I'm worried about your next year. With your current situation in mind, how can I leave you alone," he said. "Dad, what are you talking about?" asked Ali. "Nothing, my darling. I have begged God to assess my condition. I'm at the end of my rope, I cannot continue anymore," Manouchehr replied.

I calmed down, but Ali began to whimper. As soon as Ali calmed down, Hoda began to cry. Manouchehr cuddled us and said, "What can I do, as I won't be able to comfort you next Nowruz."[57] He got up and stood in

---

57. Nowruz is a big celebration of the beginning of the solar year (Iranian calendar), which is held every year on the first days of Farvardin (the first month of the Iranian calendar) in Iran and other countries that were part of ancient Iran.

front of us, "Believe me. I'm exhausted," he said. The three of us hugged him. Then, he added, "No matter if I am alive or dead, I'm with you. But the difference lies in the fact that after my death, I will be able to see you, but you won't see me. I will cuddle you, and if our souls are close together, you will feel me too."

> *How could he anticipate the hardships that lay ahead of her?! "Still, difficult days are to come…" he had said. How much could she grin and bear? An ordinary person who bore hardships due to love! Fereshteh wanted to set Manouchehr's mind at ease and said, "If you leave me alone, I will run out of patience, and I will scream around and rave. I will be dramatic, and I will complain to God." Manouchehr smiled and said, "You will have to bite the bullet."*

Why had he become cold-hearted? She couldn't comprehend that people can't live without attachments; nevertheless, they must be able to detach themselves from those attachment. He always said, "I love you too, but everything has a limit. We shouldn't pin our hopes on each other."

After the New Year's holidays, he couldn't even take a step. He had pain in his lungs, hands, and feet. It had affected his eyesight and nervous system. His body started to swell up, and as a result, his skin stretched. He couldn't even walk with the aid of a walking stick. The doctors prescribed him the last resort. To increase his body resistance, he had to receive injections that would cost 3000 dollars each. We had only two days to buy these shots. So, I had to call the Organization of Disabled War Veterans and talk to the health and treatment department manager. "First, you need to purchase the medicines and then hand over the verified prescriptions to have the money refunded," he said. I told him that we were short of money, and he replied that was our problem and then hung up.

If I wanted to sell the contents of the house, it would still come up short. It required a couple of days to sell the house and the car. I called up the Organization of Disabled War Veterans again and said, "I can't afford the medication. Send someone to get the medication. Just one day is left." He responded that it was outside of their duty. "Since that is the case, I will do something that I would rather not. You will be blamed for it in the hereafter." I asked Nader to find money no matter what, even by taking usury. We didn't let Manouchehr know about that because if he knew about it, he wouldn't take the medication. Unfortunately, the medicines didn't work.

We left the hospital and returned home. That day in the afternoon, some clerks from the Organization of Disabled War Veterans came to our house. It was unexpected for me. They reviewed Manouchehr's medical cases and said that they wanted to send him to London. "I have nothing to do in London. I feel like going to Medina, I want to go to Dokouheh, and you want to send me to London?!" Manouchehr exclaimed. They continued to insist, "If you go there, you will regain your health, and then, you can return home." Manouchehr replied, "My wife will accompany me, even if I want to go to hell," and they agreed.

I wasn't able to speak a word. We were disappointed. Manouchehr was in a severe situation, and there were only a couple of days left for us. While changing his clothes, I heard a tap on the door. Fariba came and said, "A man at the door wants to talk to Manouchehr." I wore my *chador* and went to open the door. As I opened it, a man entered the home, uttering, "*Ya Allah*."⁵⁸ I called Ali to see who the man was. But we found him sitting next to Manouchehr. Then, he put one of his hands on Manouchehr's chest and put the other hand on his head and began to pray. Ali and I were perplexed.

He turned to me, "Are you his wife?" he asked. "Yes, I am," I replied.

"Hear me out first. You should follow my orders word by word. You should recite Ziyara Ashura⁵⁹ for forty nights (and raised his right hand to confirm his words) with one-hundred curses and salutations; first start with two *rak'ah*⁶⁰ prayers for fulfillment of desires and do not speak while reciting the *ziyara*," he said.

---

58. "*Ya Allah*" (literally, O Allah) is a phrase used to address God. The term is used by Iranians as a forewarning. For example, when a stranger or non-mahram intends to enter a private place, he says "*Ya Allah*" to declare that he is about to enter the place.
59. Ziyara Ashura is a salutatory supplication addressed to Imam al-Husayn (a), the third Shiite Imam, which is recommended to be recited, particularly on the Day of Ashura (the day on which Imam al-Husayn (a) was martyred). This is widely recited by Shias, and is recommended to be recited frequently.
60. *Rak'ah* is a unit of the prayer, which includes standing (*qiyām*), rukū', and two prostrations (*sajdah*). Daily prayers consist of seventeen *rak'ahs* altogether.

I had goosebumps. As he left, I ran towards him, "Who are you? Where are you going? And where are you coming from?" I asked him. "I'm from the place where Mr. Mudeq's heart belongs," he replied. I was shaking. "You have left me with so many unanswered questions. Tell me who are you?" He smiled and said, "Look in your heart." Then, he went away.

Manouchehr laid straight with his back on the bed; he got under the duvet and then began to whimper. That day, he had a poor appetite and didn't eat or drink anything. He just recited his prayers. He insisted that I sleep and that he was fine and nothing would go wrong.

Later that night, he sat facing the *qibla*[61] and whispered until the morning. "Did I beg you to heal me, that you came to heal me? Now that you have interceded and tried to help me, I don't want to stay in this world a second longer. Prior to seeing you, I had gained courage from my family. Now that I have seen you, I don't want to stay in this world anymore." He repeated these sentences until dawn.

---

61. *Qibla* is the direction which Muslims face towards for certain acts of worship and other practices.

I couldn't contain my tears, so I said, "Manouchehr, you are very ruthless. We haven't lived together adequately. We had a hectic life. First, you were on the battlefield and then in the hospital. Let's live our lives for some more years," I begged. "Today, I saw something. If you were in my shoes, you would have wanted to leave too," he said.

We recited Ziyara Ashura for forty nights consecutively. Sometimes we even liked to go to the rooftop and recite there. He used to lie down and put his head on my lap, and I recited one-hundred curses and salutations. He kissed my hands and thanked me a lot. I focused all my attention on him. I had forgotten myself. I begged God to let him live more. Manouchehr was engrossed in his own world, whilst he was my entire world, and I only had eyes for him. It was crystal clear that he wanted to leave us.

He had become reserved and secluded. We were ready to travel. The tickets were booked, but the visas were not ready. He yearned to see his friends and bid farewell before going to London. "The time of departure is not clear yet," I said. "I don't think I will see the end of the month of

Sha'ban,[62] I am breathing my last few breaths. Something will happen this month," he said. I invited all of his friends from the ground troops and logistics. When they came, they prayed and lamented in our home. After praying, they sat around him. Manouchehr showered them with kisses. They couldn't abandon him. They left him but returned again and circled around him.

"Don't put on your shoes in haste," he said to them. I brought him a chair. As he wanted to sit on the chair, Shaykh Mehrabiyan hugged and kissed him on his head several times. "Finally, he loves someone as much as Ms. Mudeq," his friends said. "Tell us honestly, which one do you love more, Shaykh Mehrabiyan and your friends or me?" I asked Manouchehr. "I love you all the same," he replied. I asked this question three times, and his response was the same. He was sensitive about his war buddies. He was on cloud nine when he was with them. While they were leaving our home, he stood in the corridor and saw them out.

During his final days, he used to ramble most of the time, and I just listened. Once, he said, "I see my whole life like a cinema

---

62. The 8th month of Islamic lunar calendar.

screen." There was a sofa in the corner of the kitchen. He liked to sit on it and talk about his childhood while I was doing chores.

Manouchehr yearned to eat solid foods again because he had only eaten puree for many years. Fereshteh used to grind his food, even his favorite food, ghormeh sabzi, but that day he didn't want to eat puree. Fereshteh fried chunks of liver and fed him chunk by chunk. She pinched his cheeks, and they exchanged endearing words. Fereshteh's uncle, who had come to pay them a visit on the same day, said, "Hey, look at these two. They look like two lovebirds."

What makes me happy is that I loved him a lot, although I didn't express my feelings to him. Also, I wasn't embarrassed. Manouchehr said to my uncle, "I have a feeling, but I don't know how to express it. I would like to tell Fereshteh that she made me prosper in life, but I can't say it." My uncle is a poet. "Please compose a poem and read it to Fereshteh on my behalf, some days later, when I am no longer with her," Manouchehr requested him. My uncle agreed to compose a poem, "I will give that poem to you, and you yourself will read it to Fereshteh," he said. Manouchehr forced a smile on his lips but said nothing.

After that, we didn't speak a word about his departure. When I got up in the morning, my blood pressure dropped, and I had to receive a serum. When I got better, his blood pressure dropped. It looked as if he was alright, he didn't even cough. However, he had a spasm in his neck muscles and vomited. I was on edge and filled with apprehension. My stomach burned with anxiety, but I didn't think of his departure. It was midday on Tuesday when he had his lunch, but vomited blood and bile. I called Dr. Shafaeiyan, and he ordered me to take Manouchehr to the hospital at once. We got in the car and sat in the back seat. Manouchehr said to the driver, "Please wait a minute!"

His head was resting on my legs. "Raise my head," Manouchehr said. He took a glance at the home. "You will be back in a couple of days," he added, but I turned a blind eye to his words. He closed his eyes. "Have we arrived?" he asked a few minutes later. "No, we have just set off," I said. "How long has the journey become? Tell the driver to step on it," Manouchehr said. Manouchehr was fed up with the hospital. Sometimes, we twisted his arm to go to the hospital. Upon arriving, I said to the doctor, "It's no big deal. He just can't digest the food. Give him a serum, and we will return home."

"Please admit me as soon as possible," Manouchehr said.

He was bedridden in the third ward, room No. 311. He was calm as he took a glance at the bed in the room and thanked God because it was facing *qibla*. As he lay down on the bed, the color of his skin darkened. I was taken aback. He had endured the pain all the way to the hospital. I couldn't believe that he was that bad. He got better at night. "I'm feeling very sleepy, but I feel as if something sharp is piercing my heart," he said. I approached him and put my hand on his chest, and then recited al-Fateha until he fell asleep.

She couldn't recall any good memories. No matter how hard she tried to think of their good times: memories of them climbing the mountains, arm wrestling, and bantering. Manouchehr broke into laughter and told her to wait a couple of days.

She didn't need to concern herself with these things since they were supposed to return home soon.

The next morning, Manouchehr got up with a smile on his lips, but his eyes were lacking energy. "The time of departure has arrived," he said. "Stop talking about death," I told him. "Let me narrate my dream, and then you can judge whether or not you would stay in this world if you were me?" I sat next to him on the bed and clasped his hands. "I dreamt that it was Ramadan,[63] and the *iftar*[64] was ready to be served. We were ready to break our fast, and all of my martyred friends, Reza, Mohammad, Behrouz, Hassan, and Abbas, were sitting by me. I really envied them. Suddenly, someone tapped on my shoulder. It was *haj* Ebadian. 'Where were you? You have left your guests hanging!' I hugged him and said to him that I am at the end of my ropes. *haj* Ebadian put his hand on my chest and told me, 'Bid farewell to Fereshteh. Take her permission, and then you will join us, but not without her consent.'

---

63. Ramadan is the ninth month of the lunar year in which Muslims fast. It is known among Muslims as the month of God's banquet.
64. The practice of breaking the fast (*sawm*) is called *iftar*. Moreover, the meal provided for breaking the fast is also called iftar.

But I wasn't ready. "If it is in my fate, and if it is appropriate, you will have no choice but to consent!" Manouchehr said. "Weren't we supposed to be together forever?" I asked him. "Some things are out of our hands. You know I can't be far from you," Manouchehr replied.

Then, he added, "Now, I want to tell you my last words. Maybe, I will not have a chance to talk to you later. I want to speak my heart and get it off my chest. You should respond honestly," and he turned his back to me. "Do you want to propose again?!" I asked, nervously. He squeezed my hands and said, "No. This is good for both of us," and added, "I don't want you to remarry after me."

Could another person fill the void left by Manouchehr? It was an absurd notion. "Is it right to live with a person, while your soul has gone with another person?" I asked. "No," he replied. "So, it's impossible for me to remarry," I said. He turned towards *qibla* and thanked God three times from the bottom of his heart. Furthermore, he promised me to endure the separation and be patient. "I begged God to let me die as a martyr, but I don't want you and the kids to be in any trouble after my departure. Ali has grown enough to protect you and Hoda, so I'm at peace," he said.

He had shortness of breath, so I asked him to slow down to rest and catch his breath. I washed his face and hands and then combed his hair. He looked in the mirror and stroked his gray beard. He liked that his beard had grown thick and dense. He leaned on the bed and closed his eyes. The food was brought over, so I moved the serving table toward him. "No, bring that food!" he said. He pointed to the window with his finger. I didn't see anything. I put my hand on his shoulder and said, "The food is here. What are you pointing at?" He opened his eyes, "I mean that food. Why can't you see it?!" he said. He saw something that I wasn't able to see. I didn't understand his words. He lost his appetite and didn't eat anything.

Dr. Shafaeiyan called me and said, "I don't know how to say this, but Mr. Mudeq won't carry on another day. His left lung has failed. His heart has swollen, and the shrapnel is penetrating his heart."

I couldn't hold it in anymore. I cried profusely. Manouchehr was restless and couldn't find any peace on his bed. He would sit on his bed, put his head on my shoulder, and want to sleep. His whole body was racked with pain, and he could neither sleep nor sit. All of our relatives were there to pay him a visit. Hoda hugged and kissed him. She couldn't bear it anymore and said, "I can't stand this. Take me home." Fariba took Hoda home.

All of a sudden, I noticed the bloody floor of the room. The pipes of the cannula (angio) were separated from his hand and spilled onto the floor. While the nurse was bandaging his hand, the sound of the *adhan* resonated in the hospital. Manouchehr pulled himself together and sat straight, soaking his hand in his blood and stroking it to his face. "My darling, what are you doing?" I asked him. "I'm performing *wudhu* with the blood of a martyr," he replied.

He said his prayers, wrapped his hand around my neck, and then said, "Give me a hand to perform the martyrdom ablution."[65] My heart sank. "No, you may get troubled," he said while trying to calm

---

65. Martyrdom ablution or ghusl (ritual bathing) of martyrdom is a recommended ritual, which Muslim warriors performed when they anticipated they would be martyred in order to meet God in full purity.

me down.. He asked for a glass of water, and Jamshid went to fetch it. The nurse brought a pack of clothes, and we changed his clothes. Manouchehr took the glass of water intended for a martyrdom ablution and poured water over his head. His body was wet from head to toe. I lay my head in his hands, and he said, "Pray!"

I felt so perturbed that I prayed hurriedly. I recited chapter al-Fateha plus other chapters from the Quran. He laughed and said, "It's as if you are more eager to meet Allah than I am. I should be the one doing all these rituals and reciting all these verses, not you! It's as if you have reversed our roles." We hugged each other and cried. "Please, for the love of God and the sake of Sayyidah Zahra (s), detach yourself from me!" he said.

I was so selfish that I had held him only for myself. I wished for him to stay more at any price, even by taking the hardest pain. I raised my hands and said, "O God, I'm content with Your will. I don't want to see him suffer anymore." Manouchehr smiled and thanked God.

His mouth and tongue felt dry, so I poured a little water into his mouth. But he couldn't swallow it, and the water spilled out of his mouth. However, he thanked God beautifully by saying, *"Ya Husayn"*. I told Fahimeh and Mohsen to pack his belongings and take them downstairs. The nurses wanted to take him to C.C.U, so I showered him with kisses. There was a stretcher near his bed. Mohsen and I gripped Manouchehr by the waist. Ali held his feet and Nader grasped his shoulders. We helped him get up. His body was shivering and at that very moment, it was as if God answered his prayer, as he passed away in our arms and not on the hospital bed. Manouchehr did not wish to be on a hospital bed during the last moments of his life. The nurses came and took him.

> *As she got into the room, she saw Manouchehr. She closed her eyes and said, "I had the time of my life with you in different situations, and I have tolerated them because I have fallen head over heels for you, but I can't see your body in this condition anymore." She put her face to his cheeks, cried, and kissed from head to toe of Manouchehr. Then she wiped Manouchehr's face with her scarf and left the room crying.*

> *Fereshteh longed for the aroma of the earth. So, she sat on the sidewalk next to the garden near the gutter. Ali clasped her back and helped her up from the ground, and they went home. She was returning alone. The journey back home seemed to take forever. She felt that Manouchehr was waiting at home, but he wasn't. Hoda was at home. She opened the door and said, "Has daddy left this world?" Then, they hugged each other and shed tears.*

I wished for Manouchehr to be buried as soon as possible. I was concerned about his tired body. I didn't want him to stay in the morgue anymore. Manouchehr hated the cold. I looked forward to the day of the funeral, because I hadn't seen him for two days. As I saw his coffin, I got nervous to approach him. I tried to be far from him. They moved his corpse to an ambulance from the mortuary. I did not want to miss the last chance to talk to him. I knew that I wouldn't be able to see him anymore, to get the words off my chest.

Ali, Hoda, and I got in the ambulance along with some of his friends. I had wished for a long time to put my head on his chest and rest, but the shrapnel and scars on his body hindered me from doing that. I opened the shroud and looked at his face. There were some *turba* of Karbala[66] on his mouth and eyes. "It isn't fair. You have come to me with closed eyes." I longed to see his eyes, but when I removed the shroud, all I saw was the *turba* of Karbala covering them. As if Manouchehr knew my wish, the *turba* fell, uncovering the eyes I had longed to see, and I opened my heart to him. Ali and Hoda talked to him too. "You seem to be in serenity. You can sleep calmly now," I said to him. I closed his eyes and kissed him, and tied the shroud again.

I couldn't even approach his grave. I ordered the workers to look into the grave and remove the pebbles from under his face and body. After the funeral was deserted, I drew near his grave, pushed the flowers away, and laid down on his grave. I felt the same consolation Manouchehr gave me in the dust of his grave. I fell asleep there for two hours because I hadn't slept a wink for some days. From then on, I kept visiting

---

66. *Turba* or the soil of Imam al-Husayn's (a) shrine, is the soil taken from areas around the grave of Imam al-Husayn (a), the third Shiite Imam.

his grave until his fortieth.[67] When the gravestone was put on his grave, I felt the distance between us.

> *Manouchehr's photo was put up on the wall. It was his only photo in full uniform. She was expecting this moment during the day of the war, to see his photo while he became a martyr, but not now. "You have abandoned me. The visa and the ticket are ready. We should have hit the road today." Again, she couldn't hold back her tears. She felt like running away and calling Manouchehr audibly, but her voice was stuck in her throat. She ran up to the rooftop and sat on the floor, then called his name loudly from the bottom of her heart until she became calm.*

I was in a state of oblivion during the first forty days, as if the nothingness of life overwhelmed me. I didn't know whether one was coming or going. I was at the end of my tether. I knew that more difficult days were yet to come, whereby nothing would be

---

67. Fortieth or *chehellom* is a ceremony held on the fortieth day after a person's death.

able to calm me, neither visiting his grave in Beheshte-e-Zahra,[68] nor my dreams about him. One night, I went to the rooftop and communed with him in my heart. All of a sudden, a white pigeon perched itself next to me. I got angry and said, "Manouchehr, I talk to you, but you send me a pigeon?!" I went down to my room. I couldn't go to the rooftop for the next couple of days. The pigeon stayed there for a couple of days. Ali had brought it inside, but I couldn't stroke it.

Sometimes, he comes to us like a breeze and passes by my face. I recognize his fragrance. The kids recognize it too. He greets us, and we hear him. I know that he is not enjoying himself in that world, either. He is alone there, and I'm alone here. With his presence, I never experienced deep sorrow in life. But for the time being, I can't perceive the meaning of happiness. Many new things have been invented in this world, but there isn't any elixir for loneliness.

---

68. Behesht-e Zahra is Tehran's largest cemetery, where many martyrs of the Islamic Revolution, martyrs of the Iraqi war on Iran, and many other Iranian political and religious figures are buried.

www.ingramcontent.com/pod-product-compliance
Lightning Source LLC
Chambersburg PA
CBHW030041100526
44590CB00011B/289